D# 2996636

WITHDRAWN

MAR 0 9 2023

DAVID O. McKAY LIBRARY
BYU-IDAHO

D0396323

WILD VOICE OF THE NORTH

RICKS COLLEGE
REXBURG, IDAHO 83440

RICKS COLLEGE
DAVID O. McKAY LIBRARY
REXBURG, IDAHO 83440

Wild Voice of the North

BY

SALLY CARRIGHAR

Illustrated with photographs

University of Nebraska Press
Lincoln and London

Copyright © 1959 by Sally Carrighar,
Member of the Authors League of America
Copyright 1953 by the Curtis Publishing Company
All rights reserved
Manufactured in the United States of America

First Bison Book printing: 1991
Most recent printing indicated by the last digit below:
10   9   8   7   6   5   4   3   2   1

Library of Congress Cataloging-in-Publication Data
Carrighar, Sally.
Wild voice of the North / by Sally Carrighar.
p.   cm.
Reprint. Originally published: Garden City, N.Y.: Doubleday, 1959.
ISBN 0-8032-6347-3 (pbk.)
1. Bobo (Dog)   2. Siberian huskies—Alaska.   I. Title.
QL795.D6C28   1991
636.7′3—dc20
90-21044   CIP

Published by arrangement with Doubleday, a division of Bantam
Doubleday Dell Publishing Group, Inc.

♾

Other Titles by Sally Carrighar
Available in Bison Book Editions

Icebound Summer
One Day at Teton Marsh
One Day on Beetle Rock

Some of the material in this book was published in an article in The Saturday Evening Post, *illustrated by Frank Ross. Thanks are due to the editors and Mr. Ross for permission to use some of the text and photographs here. Grateful acknowledgment also is made to William W. Bacon for use of the photographs accredited to him. Other photographs are by Sally Carrighar.*

ILLUSTRATIONS

(*Following Page* 96)

WILD VOICE OF THE NORTH

1

Northern: listen to the way that Alaskans say it——

"I'm glad that they're having a Northern childhood."

"She's very Northern—seventy-one years old, still beautiful too, and feminine, and she runs the dragline out at their mine."

" . . . Reggie Joule, a real Northern pilot. He got the injured passenger into a sleeping bag and made him as comfortable as he could, and then Reggie lay down and died of his own wounds."

Northern, as used by the people who live in the arctic, has nothing to do with the frozen soil, the difficult housekeeping, prices in Fairbanks, or anything that most people elsewhere would think of as the conditions of Northern living. The clue to what it does mean is in the voice, a lightening of the tone, as if being up here in Alaska were almost too good to be true. One doesn't exult in luck like that; it is safer just to brush over it.

I have heard more than a few of the residents say, "I like winter best. Life is more Northern then." What they have in mind are the values they found in this country—but also the country itself, the white vastness, immaculate and so still, and the perfect way to get out upon it, by dog team. There is nothing in all the arctic more Northern than sled dogs.

A surprising number of the white settlers have teams. They may even have moved to Alaska because of the greater chance there to enjoy the conventional sports, such as hunting, fishing, skiing, or mountain-climbing. One mountaineer, who now lives near Fairbanks, used to say that he never felt really alive unless the place where he next put his foot determined whether he lived or died. In view from his cabin are connoisseurs' mountains, the highest anywhere on the continent —but he bought some dogs, and he does not climb so much any more. Other sportsmen have been surprised to find that their preference in outdoor recreation has now become "working a team of dogs."

"Working" a team is a prosaic phrase for an experience that can be so marvelous, one would be almost embarrassed to speak of it.

Actually there is no way except with a dog team that one can see much of the arctic in winter. The roads only go between towns and, anyway, during the cold months one's car is reluctant to move. One can fly over the landscape, but seen from the air in that season it looks very much like a black and white map. At ground level, however, the snow of the North is colored, for it reflects a long sunrise that turns imperceptibly into a long sunset: for several hours each day a sky that is gold . . . peach . . . pink . . . rose . . . magenta . . . and finally green, just before it is pricked by the stars, and the Northern Lights, cosmic ghosts, start their stately dance. Sometimes there will be a moon, the Aurora, and stars all at the same time, and all scattering smaller stars over the earth's crystal cover. There is no sound in this world, no sound whatever except the sibilance of the sled runners sliding over the snow, and the muffled pattering of the Huskies' feet, a staccato almost as soft as the fall of the snow itself.

To sharpen the nerves of the dogs and make them run faster, one can imitate lightly a ptarmigan's whistle. But most drivers, warmly encased in fur, are not in a hurry to get back home; and to judge by the dogs' alert ears and the way they continue to fling their tails about, they too would like to go farther along the white corridors in the spruce groves. If a wolf sends its call to the team, it may take some persuasion to head them back to the cabin.

As the dogs are unhitched at the door, finally, there will be new intensity in their eyes, which may mean that the voice of the wolf has aroused their own wildness. And the man hanging up the harnesses may find that his thoughts are speaking to him in a different tongue, a voice ancient and almost unknown, which nevertheless seems strangely intelligible.

Travels like these are a part of what makes the winter life Northern. But so are the strains, and they really can be a trial. The arctic cold, when it is no worse than average, is fresh and invigorating; but when it is much more severe than usual, or lasts longer, the stimulation can turn into a pathological nervousness. In the beginning this is a mild indisposition called "cabin fever." Everybody who lives in the North has at some time had a touch of it. The chief symptom is a new inclination to be alone, to stay indoors nursing a growing moroseness. When Alaskans miss one of their neighbors for several days, they suspect cabin fever and come to his aid. They invite him to dinner, take him good things to eat, surround him with so much friendliness that before long the mood is dissipated.

If it isn't, it may develop into a stage more serious, one that alarms the military as well as civilians. Several years ago three enlisted men were stationed up on the barren coast about seventy-five miles north of Nome. The three were congenial and seemed to be getting along very well at their lonely post. One of their pastimes was play with a tame squirrel that came into their cabin. Two of the men were gone for several hours one day, and when they returned they found that the third man had shot the squirrel. He was as mystified as the others as to his reason. The killing of the pet was reported in the daily radio conversation with headquarters, and the one who had done it was whisked away from the site as fast as a plane could get there. The officers knew that more serious violence had become a danger.

The disturbance into which cabin fever may grow is the widely known "going berserk." "Berserk" is a Scandinavian word for *bear shirt* and refers to legendary Norse warriors, dressed in bear skins, who sometimes went mad in battle. "Berserksgangr" is a phenomenon in all arctic lands. The disturbed mental state is not well understood, but it would seem to merit much more attention. In the arctic at least it appears that there is a connection between some violent crimes and weather.

The first winter I spent in Alaska was the most rigorous in twenty-two years. The cold continued a month longer than normally, with more storms, coming closer together. Out on the coast of the Bering Sea ten blizzards struck in a period of six weeks—so the Weather Bureau reported. They overlapped and to us seemed like one blizzard six weeks long. Two people at Kotzebue froze to death only a dozen feet from their door, unable to find it; native hunters were lost on the sea ice; and an old man who fell on an icy path near the center of Nome died of the cold before he was discovered. Six planes, trying to get through the snow-blows, crash-landed.

Besides hazards directly due to the weather, "berserks-gangr" became a threat. In Nome there were several unprovoked attacks, and one murder so frightful that some women barricaded themselves in their houses, refusing to go outside even during the daytime. No crimes were committed in the Eskimo village where I was staying, but I noticed a growing tendency to talk about cases of Eskimos' going berserk in the past.

To me as a naturalist it was very significant that a growing nervousness in the sled dogs paralleled that of the people. The dogs also had had to endure too many storms for one year, and most of them had been tied outdoors through the worst of the weather. They huddled as far as they could into their furry coats, and almost invariably were snappish when roused. Was that stage the equivalent of cabin fever in people? Next came the attacks. In one town a team jumped the girl teacher, whose life was saved only because a young Eskimo woman rushed into the pack of maddened, ferocious animals and somehow was able to drive them off. And at Unalakleet the team pulling a sled on which I was riding attacked a man for no reason that one could see, except possibly that the dogs went berserk.

All in a few hours, then, the cold, difficult days were past and the brief arctic summer arrived. As always, its coming seemed like an explosion of warmth. For the start of the summer is timed with the sailing away of the sea ice, and that's an event which can take place overnight.

I was in Nome that year when the ice went out. For more than eight months the white field had spread west on the ocean. The needed supply ship was anchored down by the mouth of the Yukon, where it was blocked by the ice. The Eskimos' skin boats could not take them out on their walrus hunts. Every day, as the climbing sun melted the surface, the ice became shinier and more glaring, but it continued to chill the air that otherwise would be growing warm.

Finally, under a strong wind, the ice broke at the shore. It drifted away in a sheet and was gone from sight the next morning. Now the chunks and knobs of ice dammed up in rivers could begin pouring out into the sea. All moving along at exactly the same speed, they passed by the beach at Nome like a flotilla of little ships. Sparkling and iridescent, they were a beautiful sight, but they too held back the summer.

At last their white hulls disappeared over the northern horizon. Then the sea looked less deeply blue. Smooth as it was, the water seemed flattened by soft opalescent light, swirling in oily patterns. The sun set in the north about midnight and rose, again in the north, only an hour later. All the rest of the time it poured down its heat.

There were many chores to be done before the next winter. Hammers would chime on the August air. Rusted stovepipes would be replaced; windows, loosened by wind, would be nailed tight again; doors would be squared, and new shingles patch up the old. But July was a recess. Until one absorbed the experience of the break-up, there was no impulse to start preparing for the next freeze-up.

Everything was now warm to the touch: the doorknob, the

porch rail, and underfoot the old boardwalks and dust of the unpaved streets. Warmth in the arctic: everyone drenched himself in the good sensation. Men would start to walk from their offices to the bank and find themselves stopped in front of the first sunny wall. Women en route to the market dropped down on a bench on Front Street and hours later would not have moved. After nearly nine months when the ocean was frozen, there was a kind of hypnosis in hearing the breakers, in seeing them splash between walls on the other side of the street. Let the stovepipe fall down, let a blown door stay open, let the weather-stripping come loose—these were no longer emergencies. Let the roast wait till tomorrow.

That was the season and mood on a day when I was one of the bench-sitting women. The other occupant was an Eskimo with a baby saddled against her back. The woman sat upright, as Eskimos do, seemingly with no strain, her placid frame being its own support. And the day was still, basking in dreamy peace. No car moved in the road.

I looked at the woman's hands, which lay in her lap, capable hands now at ease, their palms turned to the sun. Suddenly they gripped shut. It was a gesture of fear. I followed the woman's glance and discovered a pack of seventeen dogs rounding a corner to come onto Front Street.

The dogs weren't relaxed. Heading towards us and nearly filling the road, they moved with electric intensity. The Huskies did; two or three were of other breeds, and those dogs seemed more to be just amusing themselves till the time when their dinners appeared automatically in their rubber dishes. Huskies, so recently of wolf blood, still have not lost the sense that they must find their food if they are going to eat. Most of these Huskies were well-fed dogs, yet the old anxiety tightened their nerves. They were like the wild hunters.

Most were Malemutes, with the black "mask" across their eyes. They were losing their winter coats. The fur had come out in patches, showing the darker fur beneath and making the dogs unkempt and ragged-appearing. But all of their tails were up over their backs, proudly, and thrashing from side to side.

The dogs' motion was like the wind's, now streaming ahead, now whipping into a knot, sweeping this way and that, with its moments of immobility. And over it all were the swish and brush of the waving plumes: an arresting sight, slightly fearsome but a spirited thing to see.

The loitering human figures along sunny walls had slipped into the stores. The street was empty except for the dogs and the two of us on the bench. We hadn't had time to go in anywhere, we were sitting too near the corner. We could only remain there, as inconspicuous as we could make ourselves.

However the dogs grouped themselves, their formation flowed towards a point—their leader. He was not the largest dog, but was the only Siberian of the seventeen—a black, gray, and white Husky whose winter coat had shed evenly, so that he still was sleek. The white fur was very white: a ruff over his shoulders, which caught the sun like a halo, and a white muzzle, chest, legs, and feet. His tail too fanned out into white, and he carried the tail so high that it made an arc over his back.

He was reconnoitering. First he stopped at a paper bag near the edge of the walk and, steadying it with a paw, tore it open. While he sniffed at the contents the other dogs stood aside. Whatever it held, the Siberian did not want it. He left it, and some of the others closed in to examine the bag, but most of them turned away, falling in again after the leader.

He appeared to be taking an interest in everything, not only possible food and the scent posts. A bit of green rag in the dust and a child's broken plastic toy were worthy of his attention. Doubtless the dog knew this street very well, and these were objects not previously examined. The green rag and the toy had been on the other side of the road, and, with the pack concentrated around them, it seemed that the Eskimo and I were going to escape the dogs' notice. But the leader now lifted his nose and, after a second's pause, headed across to our side. The other dogs, sensing a definite purpose, drew together and followed more closely behind him.

As the leader came near, I could see that his eyes were a strong, clear blue, the blue that is found in most wolf puppies and among the adult Siberian Huskies. The leader had also the rather short legs and powerful chest that are typical of his strain: it is the massive chest muscles that give the Siberians their superior pulling power. Siberians are sought, too, for their stamina—"They will go seventy-five miles on one little fish, twice as far as a Malemute," one Eskimo told me; but most of all they are prized for their eager temperament. Siberians could be called the perfectionists among dogs. On a trail they try so earnestly to perform well that they sometimes burst blood vessels and dislocate joints. These things I had been told in Unalakleet, although no one there owned Siberians. And so now I was watching this lead dog with particular interest and the pleasure one takes in any superior creature.

Happily we were not the lure that had brought him across the street. That was no more than the heel of a woman's shoe, torn off when it caught in a crack of the boardwalk. No doubt he had smelled the leather, for now he not only sniffed it but pulled it out. After chewing on it a moment, he tossed it and caught it and tossed it—but another dog moved in and, when the heel came down, jumped for it.

This dog was a large and ungainly mongrel. The Siberian stiffened. His fur seemed to give off sparks. He did not growl, but with a tense step he approached the mongrel and tried to put his head over the other's neck.

The meaning was evident: an assertion of his authority, and even though the Siberian looked a little ridiculous, not being as tall as the mongrel and therefore not able to get his chin all the way over, the gesture was nevertheless successful. The other dog dropped the heel. The Siberian tossed it up one more time and then let it lie where it fell and roamed away, now with a manner even a little more jaunty.

Never far from the leader, and apparently most devoted, was a white, short-haired Husky, not a very bright-looking dog. His gait had less pride than some of the others', and of course the Siberian's, and his eyes were less wary. He seemed amusingly like a bodyguard, a role that would suit him well, for he was a huge dog—the largest.

Once, as the pack turned away from some disappointing discovery, the white dog was out ahead. He continued in that position for several yards—until suddenly, with a dash of speed, the Siberian made a long forward leap. It took him diagonally across the white Husky's path, and, as he shot by, he turned his muzzle and brushed it along the other dog's face. Was the leader again asserting authority, and now not in a domineering way, since the white dog apparently was his friend?

At the next side street the dogs swung away from the beach, out of sight, with the Siberian still in front and stepping along, plainly assured of his dominance.

The hands of the Eskimo opened out again in her lap. She said, "Dogs run in packs like that, sometimes attack people."

"I know. I've been living in Unalakleet for a year, and down there the Eskimos warned me to get off the trail if a team was coming. 'Always keep out of the way of the teams,' they said."

"We do that. Every place."

I was going to tell her about the attack I had seen, but I realized that she knew the danger—why increase her fear? All I said then was, "That's a beautiful dog, that Siberian. He didn't look mean."

"He is nice dog. He is family dog. I know the people that own him. If he could hold back other dogs, they would not attack."

If he could hold back the other dogs—yes, if he could.

That might be expecting too much of even the strongest leader.

2

Fate was starting to do some weaving for the blue-eyed Siberian Husky. Not immediately, but within a year, his life would have a new pattern composed of three strangely assorted threads: lemmings, a gaunt gold-rush house, and myself. These, none of which now concerned him, would be determining whether he might survive. But before the threads could be put together they had to be spun, and that process would take a little time.

If the Husky had been a sled dog instead of a "family dog," lemmings would have been very familiar to him. Those small arctic rodents are the most relished food of the Northern wolves and therefore of Huskies, who share the inheritance of the wolves. When a lemming scent crosses the trail of a team of dogs, even a very dependable leader may swing off to follow it, although some leaders will fake an interest in other, imaginary scents to divert the team's attention. The flesh of lemmings is so palatable, in fact, that lemmings are eaten roasted by people in some parts of Northern Europe. An Alaska bush pilot who had crash-landed up on the arctic slope saved his life by subsisting on lemmings during the three weeks before he was found.

A lemming hunt was my own reason for stopping at Nome

that summer. For a year I had been in the North in order to gather material for a book about arctic animals. Many are rare and little-known species, and heading the list as the most important were lemmings.

The significance of the little animals is both scientific and literary. Few biologists ever have seen them, although lemmings are a key species and determine the populations of many others. Their effect is due to the way they increase explosively and then, in companies numbering millions, migrate down to the sea and drown. So few are left that one could believe they had become extinct; but again, in only three or four years, they have reached their fantastic density.

During the time when so many of them are available, a whole group of predators live on little else—and being so well fed, themselves breed at an abnormal rate. Other creatures like squirrels and hares, that ordinarily would be prey, are left alone, and they too increase. Wolves ignore caribou, which they hunt at other times, when their hunger is satiated with lemmings. The results extend a long way from the arctic. Snowy owls, a far Northern species, thrive and multiply at the peak of the lemmings' cycle. When they can find no more lemmings, the owls' hunger takes them south even into the Carolinas—and small birds and mammals there become the victims of owls they otherwise never would see.

For their importance biologically, then, lemmings had aroused my curiosity, especially since no scientist ever has given an undisputed explanation of why they go on their suicidal migrations (suicidal in effect, if not in intention). Some biologists are convinced that the lemming hordes leave their birthplace because they have exhausted the mosses and grass in those areas. Examinations of lands over which they have passed, however, have proved that much nourishment still may be there.

For centuries it has been part of the folklore of Europe to believe that the migrating lemmings were seeking a former home on the lost Atlantis or, to speak scientifically, on lands which existed during the Miocene period and now are covered by parts of the North Sea and Baltic Sea. I don't know of any biologists who take that theory seriously—although they do sometimes speculate as to whether the northward migrations of birds every spring could be due to the birds' racial memories of arctic homes in the distant past.

But the legends aren't all found in Europe. In every far Northern country, on every continent, the primitive people call lemmings "mice from the sky." The Eskimo word is *kay-loong-meu-tuk*. Several serious-minded Eskimos told me of seeing the lemmings come down, "falling in bigger and bigger circles that turned same way as sun" or, as we would say, clockwise. Eskimos who had not seen the lemmings descend all could describe lemming tracks that "start where the lemmings landed, without any footprints going out to that place." The late Reggie Joule, an Eskimo bush pilot and son of intelligent native teachers, said that the familiar spurs of lemming tracks often are found on the roofs of the Eskimo cabins at Point Hope, where he grew up, "and there weren't any tracks outside the cabins." He concluded, "I think lemmings fly."

The more common Eskimo explanation is that lemmings float down to the earth from some distant star. (The very smallest spacemen—and Eskimos have prehistoric beliefs about flying saucers or, as they say, flying baskets, but the lemmings weren't passengers. It is believed that they drift down freely.)

I did not take the stories about the tracks very seriously—until a day when I had a chance to see some of them for myself. It was early in April when Frank Ryan, the Eskimo postmaster at Unalakleet, told me that lemmings had landed that day, from the sky of course, on the end of the airstrip. I hurried out. The blacktop was covered with less than an inch of new, light, soft snow—too shallow for any lemming to tunnel under it without thrusting up a ridge on the surface. And there, indeed, were the mysterious little trails, just as the Eskimos had described them. In fifteen places a track began rather faintly for a couple of inches, as if an animal had come down and gently coasted onto the snow. The tracks then continued more deeply, the individual footprints showing clearly, and also the slight brush marks between the footprints where the hairs on the lemmings' feet dragged. They were not mouse tracks, for then there would have been a tail mark between the footprints; but lemmings have only half-inch tails, which they carry turned up as they run. In each case the tracks led off the blacktop to a clump of grass, where the lemming evidently had burrowed down among the roots.

And how could those tracks just begin suddenly, out there on the smooth white surface? I have no idea. Lemmings cannot jump even a fraction as far. They have no membranes between their forelegs and hind legs, as bats have, and therefore they cannot fly. They do have long, soft, thick fur, and briefly I wondered if the wind could have picked up the fluffy little creatures and set them down on the airstrip. That possibility would have been reasonable, perhaps, if the wind had been strong enough on that day to have drifted the snow.

It wasn't; the snow was as light as eiderdown and it lay as level as it had fallen. That owls did not pick up the lemmings as they were venturing out on the surface is obvious because the tracks led *to* the clumps of grass, not away from them. An owl (owls and ravens were the only large birds present in the North in that month) might have dropped one squirming lemming—but hardly fifteen in a space about twenty yards square. Naturally I do not believe that the lemmings arrived from a distant star. But the tracks and some other mysteries that developed later remain just that: mysteries, and I don't belittle the Eskimos for devising what must have seemed a logical explanation for them.

I had been trying to find some live lemmings ever since I first came to Alaska. I wanted to take a colony of them to San Francisco, where they were going to be housed and studied by others besides myself at the California Academy of Sciences. Unfortunately I had arrived in the North during the crash period of the lemming cycle, and they had proved very elusive. All the natives at Unalakleet, where at times lemmings are very common, knew I was hunting for them, and six had been seen by various people who tried to capture them, unsuccessfully. In fact, my need for lemmings had been publicized throughout Alaska, and many others were looking for them. The fact that no lemmings were found showed how scarce they were at the sag in their cycle, but when I saw the tracks out at the airfield, late that afternoon, I thought that my problem was solved. Wherever they came from, at least and at last they were here. In the morning I'd dig up the grass roots where they had gone, and I felt certain that I would find them.

By morning I had a fast-developing case of pneumonia and,

as soon as a mercy plane could be sent, was bound for Nome and the hospital. It was another instance of the frustration that had characterized the lemming hunt all through the year. When I returned to Unalakleet a month later, the lemmings had vanished, leaving only a few little dried-out pellets which could be identified and which proved that they had, indeed, been there temporarily.

There was new hope, however. On the day that I left the hospital I had met, at Nome, an Air Force major who told me the welcome news that there were "thousands" of lemmings on St. Lawrence Island. They were "running all over the place," he said. A geologist, he had been out on the island surveying an airfield, and, since he was a scientist, I felt sure I could trust his word. In July, then, I was back at Nome, with the objective of getting myself to St. Lawrence Island.

The island lies out in the Bering Sea within view of the coast of Siberia. Its principal Eskimo settlement, Gambell, is 210 air miles from Nome. No commercial planes or ships made the trip in that summer, but the Air Force and Navy went out very often and sometimes they took civilians, who had no other way of getting there. The major assured me that the Air Force would give me a lift. By July he himself had gone back to the States.

The Air Force, when interviewed at Nome, refused my request for a ride. The Navy also refused. I explained the project to numerous officers, who listened with patience but little sympathy, and persisted in calling the lemmings mice. Radio messages flew back and forth between Nome and more distant headquarters, but the answers were all the same: catching some mice was not considered a need urgent enough to breach the security program.

By the end of July I had given up hope of reaching that island where lemmings were running all over. I would return to San Francisco, my base, and make another trip to the arctic the following summer. It was a disappointing and an expensive compromise, and the work of the winter would be handicapped by having no firsthand knowledge of the significant lemmings. But there seemed to be no other choice.

3

Very briefly, during this trying experience with the military, I had thought of the Coast Guard. During the ice-free months a Coast Guard cutter cruises around in the northern Alaska waters. There, where no lifesaving stations or lighthouses are maintained, other ships do at times need the cutter's help. Besides standing by for emergencies, it is one of the peacetime duties of the Coast Guard "to send a cutter to remote parts of the Alaskan coast to carry medical aid and the benefits of law and civilization to the whites and natives." Wouldn't a survey of arctic wildlife be one of the benefits of civilization? I thought so and had inquired whether the cutter might be making a trip to St. Lawrence and was told, by an Army officer, that the cutter might indeed go, but except for rescue work no woman had been allowed on a Coast Guard ship for eight years. The ban was due to the fact that one woman, permitted to ride on the cutter for a short distance, had refused to get off. For several months she thus avoided a legal summons from a husband who wished to divorce her.

I therefore abandoned all hope of the Coast Guard too, without knowing that officers of the cutter then in the arctic, the *Clover*, had heard the radio messages about the woman who wanted "mice," and had felt that the other services were a little ungallant, and had wanted to come to my aid. The director of the Guggenheim Foundation, which was financing my project, also had presented the problem to the commandant; but unaware that wheels, or rather propellers, had started to turn, I left Nome, bound for Kotzebue, where I planned to take a plane out of Alaska.

On the way to Kotzebue I stopped over at the Eskimo hamlet of Shishmaref for the year's final lemming hunt. When the bush plane came down on the beach, several natives gathered to greet the pilot, and they had reassuring answers to my questions about the lemmings. Not thousands but maybe hundreds of them had been seen on the sand dunes since spring —some within the last week. The plane left and I hired an Eskimo with a shovel.

Few human settlements anywhere have as slight a toehold in nature's impersonal element as Shishmaref. Its residents speak of living on an island, but it's only a sandbar, really, with a few acres of beach grass. Yet the scene is attractive in a spacious and airy way—this stretch of sand all surrounded by water as clean, clear, and blue as if it were the earth's first, original sea.

The Eskimo, Foster Olanna, and I walked to the eastern tip of the island, then back from the shore to low mounds of salt-green sedges and cotton grass. Everywhere they were crisscrossed with little trails, used so lately that the new shoots of grass on the floor of the trails showed only as pale yellow tips. The runways led to the burrow entrances, which were up on the sides of the mounds, Foster said, in order to be above the spring meltwater that would lie in the dune trenches. He started to dig out the tunnels, while I stood poised with a butterfly net to capture the lemmings as they might run out.

The burrows were intricate, curving passages up to a dozen feet long, all interconnected and with chambers opening off to the right and left. In each network one "room" was used exclusively for the animals' droppings. Some of the others were filled with the empty casings of grass stems, cut in three-quarter-inch lengths, amazingly uniform. These seemed to serve as padding for nests after the nourishment in the stem had been eaten. Outside the burrows Foster pointed out many stubs of stems, cut off just above the rootstocks. When he would be walking over the snow on his snowshoes in winter, he said, he often had seen a stalk of grass suddenly shrink and disappear as some lemming beneath had pulled it down through the snow and run away with it to the burrow.

We excavated a dozen or more of the tunnel communities —little ghost towns from which every resident had departed. To go where? Since this was a small, narrow island, the only direction the lemmings could have taken was towards the sea. They could only have crossed the wide, smooth beach, festooned at the tide marks with flowerlike shells—a migration of two hundred yards, but a death march.

Why?

The burrows looked comfortable, and the runways the lemmings had made in the sunny grass led through food that was still abundant. In what way were their lives so intolerable that they gave them up? What seemingly "unnatural" instinct overcame the instinct of self-preservation, so that young and old took themselves out of this pleasant place to enter the cold salt waves?

Now, more than ever, I felt I must find some live lemmings

—capture enough to have a colony of them, keep them where I could see them continuously as I was working, and hope that they would reveal some hint of the curious impulse that destroyed them. Certainly I would come back the following summer. The population of lemmings should have begun to increase by then.

And would the walls of a cage, if not their own wish to survive, force them to live? For how long? A project like this has avenues opening out and out.

While I was waiting at Shishmaref for the return of the bush pilot, I heard the most whimsical of the numerous lemming legends. It concerned the white species. Of two closely related lemming strains, one remains brown in all seasons, whereas the other, whose members climb up out of the snow to eat the bark of berry bushes, turns white in the winter—no doubt an example of nature's camouflage. Carson, the Eskimo storekeeper, told this little story about the white lemmings, as we were sitting outdoors in the crisp arctic sunshine.

He had been talking about the Little People, who "used to come down from the clouds all the time, but we don't see them so much any more." I asked if they came to help human beings, and he said, "No, they just come to visit, but sometimes they do something friendly. One winter day some of them came ashore from the sea ice and told the people that they'd seen a lot of the white polar bears out there. The hunters got their harpoons and the Little People led them to the place on the ice where they'd seen the bears. But they weren't bears, they were only white lemmings, which looked big to the Little People because they are small. The men hit the lemmings this way and that with their spears: 'That's how we kill your polar bears,' they said.

"The Little People came back to the shore, and we saw them making harpoons for themselves. Then they went out on the ice to try to kill their own bears. Pretty soon they found some, and they tried to knock them out the same way they'd seen the men do—only these were real polar bears and they turned on the Little People and chased them. They would have caught them, too, but the Little People took themselves back to the clouds in a hurry."

With my bags on the plane at Kotzebue and forty minutes to wait before it would leave—there, too, still looking for lemmings, I went for a walk. A boat pulled up on the beach and a sailor jumped out.

"Can you tell us where to find Sally Carrighar?" he asked. "We have come to take her to St. Lawrence Island."

When the plane soared up from Kotzebue, I was in the boat, on my way to the *Clover*, which was anchored twelve miles out to sea.

There were signs of a gale approaching. I had been out in other storms on these Northern waters and was glad that I need not dread this one—for in what ship, if not a Coast Guard cutter, could one ever experience, intimately and yet securely, the ocean's wild fury? As it happened, the cutter's radar equipment went out of commission. Our route led along the arctic coast and down through Bering Strait into the Bering Sea, but the strait is a treacherous channel, strewn with rocky islands and approached past a shoal that has wrecked many ships. Without radar Captain Shannon did not wish to risk the passage, not in the racing fog and tremendous waves that soon were whipped up. Therefore we headed north, straight for the North Pole, in waters where there was little chance of collision with any other ship, though we might be encountering ice floes. The waves were as big as the cutter itself, and I said to one of the officers, "Even you will admit that this is rough water?" And he laughed: "Yes, I'd say this is almost a full sea."

A full sea: wonderful phrase! I took it to mean that the waves were about as high as waves ever become.

Due to the storm it took us four days to travel the four hundred miles from Kotzebue to the island. By the end of that time all the men on board had become interested in lemmings, and from one, Chet Frogle, the chief engineer, I learned something that may clear up one of the lemming mysteries.

While I was in Kotzebue an Eskimo woman had told me that once, when she had caught a lemming "coming down from the sky," she killed it and cut open its stomach, which was filled with very fine grass, bright green, she said. "And it was winter, when nothing is green down here, so that lemming came from a star."

Engineer Frogle, hearing this tale in the wardroom at dinner one night, said, "The green stuff in their stomachs is probably dried grass turned green by the action of the stomach juices. I was brought up on a farm, and I know that after a cow eats hay it turns back into green grass in her stomach."

A radio message had been sent ahead from the ship to the St. Lawrence weather station, asking that some Eskimos be employed to catch lemmings before our arrival. The next day a report came back that two or three dozen lemmings were caged in some boxes on the beach.

We anchored late in the morning in the channel between St. Lawrence Island and the Siberian coast. It is always a turbulent strip of water and that day the waves were about fifteen feet high. Nevertheless, an Eskimo skin boat came alongside while we were having lunch. The men in the *umiak*, more enterprising than some of their neighbors, had brought out their ivory carvings to sell in advance to the crew. The *umiak* was hoisted up onto the deck, and when the officers and I went out, Captain Shannon said to the natives, "We have brought Sally Carrighar to your island to get some lemmings. And we hear by radio that you've caught some of them and they're on the beach."

"On the beach, all right," said one of the Eskimos. "Only —not lemmings."

Stunned by a terrible premonition, I said, "No *kay-loong-meu-tuk?* I was told there are thousands—'running all over,' a scientist said."

"Maybe few *kay-loong-meu-tuk* back in mountains some place. I never see any here. I see them on mainland one time, different from what we catch for you. Little animals, run every place on St. Lawrence Island, just mice."

I looked around at the faces of all these men who had spent four days bringing me here on this ship, and I remembered the woman who had duped the Coast Guard eight years before, and all I could gasp was, "Right now I would risk my life to find lemmings."

It's the kind of thing that one shouldn't say, because fate takes us up on those proclamations.

The captain was courteous and kind. He apparently was convinced that I had been given the wrong information and that I almost was overcome with embarrassment. We went ashore to make sure that the captive animals were not lemmings, and they were indeed mice, tundra voles, of which I already had kept more than a dozen caged at Unalakleet, for months. I paid the mouse-hunters and we returned in the launch to the ship.

The *Clover* is not only a cutter but an ice-breaker, with a bowl-shaped hull so that her prow can be driven up on the sea ice to break it. Because of the ship's incurving sides, the Jacob's ladder for mounting up to the open deck dangled loose in the air for ten to fifteen feet, and swayed in and out with the roll of the ship in this channel. It had not been hard to go down it—one could just drop off the end into the launch below, but getting onto a Jacob's ladder isn't easy for anyone when the water is very rough. I had already heard about one of the seamen who had lost his life a month earlier as he tried to board the Coast Guard weather ship in the Aleutian Trough. The captain warned me therefore to jump onto the ladder fast, when a wave would lift the launch to its fullest height—and I tried. My hands caught the ropes at the sides of the ladder, but my rubber-soled shoepaks slipped off the wet bottom rung. There I hung, with the extra handicap of a large press camera suspended around my neck between me and the ladder. With the ladder swinging so widely my feet could not find the rung again quickly, and I didn't dare try to drop into the launch because, strung up as I was, I couldn't look down. I could look up, though, and I saw the faces of several crew members peering over the edge of the deck. All were taut and some even quite pale, and their concern struck me as very nice and also a little humorous, and helped me to keep my head until I could get and keep my feet back on the ladder.

The ship was to take me to Nome. As we steamed away from St. Lawrence I was not only troubled about the fruitless outcome of this generous effort—although the officers had assured me that they were in the North on a standby basis and might as well be going out to the island as anywhere; but also, what about the reaction of the Nome officers in the other services? They, who had insisted on calling lemmings mice and had refused their help in securing them: how now would they comment on the courteous gesture made by the officers of the *Clover?* Those were my unhappy musings—but only till midnight. At that time we sailed into the center of a scene so rare that, as far as I know, no other naturalist ever has had a chance to observe it.

I was up on the bridge as we moved along in the arctic's unearthly twilight, surrounded by silence so vast that even the sound of the engines seemed hushed . . . when there ahead we discovered a carnival of the giant humpback whales playing. More than a dozen were rolling about in the waves, chasing each other, diving up into the air to descend in slow, graceful arcs, with often a frolicsome toss of their flukes just before the water closed over them. Theirs was the most complete release of high spirits I ever had seen, by some of the largest animals in existence, on one of the most remote seas.

The ensign on duty signaled for slower speed, and the cutter slipped into the very center of the whales' playground. Yet the whales, all around us now, continued to tumble. Possibly they were too possessed with joy to conceive of danger arising from this other, even more massive bulk.

It was hard to think of the whales as animals. They were so huge they seemed almost cosmic, as if this were nature itself at play—free and spontaneous and entirely benign. I wished the ensign and I had not been the only ones watching. I wished everyone who thinks of nature in tooth-and-claw terms could have been there on the ship, for none could have failed to see the innocence of that play, innocent as play only is when it arises from the heart's impulse.

The whales were still splashing and diving, their immense bodies so light, when we left them, when the ship, trailing its thin, long line of smoke, disappeared eastward beyond their horizon.

This undreamed-of opportunity to be in the very midst of the animals in their unguarded gambols—not hunted, not migrating, just amusing themselves as if humans didn't exist—was the climax of the entire year I had then spent in the arctic. Lemmings could and would be found elsewhere, but only the trip to St. Lawrence provided the prize.

I would write about it, of course. The play of the whales would become some of the most important material in the book about Northern wildlife. Meanwhile, leaving the bridge, I decided to spread that word around rather widely while I was in Nome, hoping it might reach the ears of any inclined to facetiousness at the expense of the Coast Guard.

4

While I was waiting for a taxicab on the dock, I talked to Arnot Castel, a gusty little Frenchman who owns a small boat, something like a tug, in which he scampers around the Alaska coast in the summer, picking up and delivering freight. I had met him at Unalakleet and now told him my lemming troubles.

"Let me take you to Barrow!" he urged. "You can always get lemmings at Barrow!"

"Thousands—just like St. Lawrence Island?" I said it laughing.

"No! Real lemmings! I know! I have lived at Barrow."

For a few moments I thought I would go—to be truthful, until I remembered the mountainous seas that had heaved up and dropped the *Clover*. What would Castel's little boat do in such waters? I didn't care to find out. But during the conversation I did decide that I would try Barrow first when I came back the next summer. I knew Arnot Castel's reputation, and if he said lemmings were there, I was sure they would not turn out to be voles.

I reserved a seat on a plane that was going to Fairbanks that evening and then went into the hotel dining room for a cup of tea. Alma, the redheaded girl in charge, came and sat down at my table. Always vivacious, that day she was fairly giddy and told me why: she and her husband had just bought a house. They had been coming to Nome for several summers, working a claim they owned out on one of the creeks and always dreaming that they would find gold enough so they could stay. They had a devotion to Nome that was almost fanatical—a curious but familiar attitude. This summer had seen their dream realized. With a very good season's take, they had purchased one of the old gold-rush "mansions" and were starting to work on it. "It's a wreck but nice." And was I going outside? Leaving Nome? Alma was puzzled by anyone who could be immune to the fascination of this so-distant, small mining town.

She continued to sit at the table and share her exhilaration: "It's the craziest house you ever saw. In the middle of the master bedroom there's a bathtub eight feet long. Nobody knows what for, because there isn't any plumbing upstairs and you couldn't fill it by carrying up a teakettleful of water at a time.

"We'll have to have the house leveled. The Nome houses get tipped by the permafrost—you know? We threw a handful of marbles down on the living room floor and they all rolled to one corner. That's the way people here see if their houses need jacking up.

"I guess it's the only house in Nome that has wallpaper. You can't put wallpaper on walls that are twisting around all the time, but this wallpaper is pasted on cloth that's hung from the ceiling. Fifteen layers. I peeled them off in one corner to see what the paper's been like all these years. The last layer, the gold-rush paper, was white with gilt bowknots and bright pink roses. We're just painting the paper, white on the walls, dark green on the ceiling, white woodwork. There's a genuine silver picture molding, but we're painting that, too."

"Is the house very big?" I asked her. I hadn't seen any really large house in Nome.

"Big enough if you have to heat it—six good-sized rooms and four storerooms. One of the storerooms has outside ventilation—a game cache. It's fitted up to store a whole winter's meat—caribou, moose, mountain sheep, ptarmigan, salmon strips. My husband thinks that he's going to fill it."

It certainly sounded like frontier living—rather inviting. But the fifteen layers of paper and tilted floors?

Having several hours to spend before taking the plane, I walked up to see Alma's house. The mild envy I'd felt turned into sympathy at the vast amount of work, and the investment, that would be needed to make the house livable. Had Alma not seen the gaps where the shingles were gone, the rusted-out stovepipes, weathered door, and the sagging steps?

A small Eskimo boy joined me and said in a tone of something like awe,

"That's a castle."

"Oh? It does look a little like one—with that sort of tower." The "tower" had two round windows in it. "Did you ever see a princess smiling out of one of the tower windows?" He looked so puzzled that I realized "princess" is not in an Eskimo child's vocabulary. "A princess is just a very nice girl. The daughter of a chief."

"No, but Tommy's going to move in tomorrow," said the child. "Maybe he'll look at me out of the windows."

The dear Eskimos, I thought; I shall remember them always.

And indeed I shall, for I was to see much more of them than I expected that afternoon when I thought I was taking my leave of them.

As I was turning away, a white furred muzzle appeared in the entrance of the house beyond Alma's. With extreme wariness it moved farther out: a pair of lucent blue eyes, and the black head and white ruff of the Siberian Husky dog. He stopped and peered keenly to one side and the other, an advance so cautious that it reminded me of a deer approaching the edge of a clearing. Finally, finishing his survey of the street, the dog stepped down onto the boardwalk.

We stood facing each other—his intensity so much greater than mine, intensity of the kind that always startles us in the wild. It was not the same quality as the high-strung nervousness of the very specialized breeds of dogs, a nervousness which builds up from emotions within the creature. The sensitivity of the Husky was at the other end of the dog scale: the utter stillness that goes with a wild animal's total skepticism of the unknown. The dog had quieted every impulse except that of perceiving this strange human being. It was an instinct like that of the deer, of an otter I once surprised as she was entering her burrow, and of parent trumpeter swans, when I came out of a woodland border onto the shore of a lake where they guarded cygnets.

There was this difference: no wild animal would have held his gaze on my face for so long. The wild ones are very shy of the moment when an exchange between eyes proceeds from observing to become communication. They are so disturbed by that other element that if one continues to stare at them, they often show the beginning of panic, and dash away or attack. But this Husky had no embarrassment and no dread of that borderline. His arresting eyes, steady, unwavering, stayed on my own until I was the one who felt the tension and had to break it. I dropped my glance to the child's face, and asked, "What is the name of the dog?"

"He's Bobo," said the boy, and draped himself over the Husky's back and ran his blunt little fingers through the white, long-furred ruff.

"He's Sonny's dog. He always play with us. I like him."

Bobo let himself down on the boardwalk slowly, with controlled grace like a cat's, and when I looked back at his face, his eyes still held on my own but they seemed only curious now.

I felt that I almost could go up and stroke this milder-appearing dog; almost, not quite. I was sure Bobo would not tolerate that kind of patronizing. Descendant of wolves, he had the wild nature but, in addition, some great canniness inherited from the dog side of his ancestry, and with that canniness he could forestall any familiarity that he did not want. Eskimos have been breeding their sled dogs for centuries for that spirit of independence, as well as for wolves' sensitivity. How extraordinary it would be, I thought as I left, to own one of these Huskies, to have the wild instincts, the wild reactions, applied to one's everyday human life! It was an opportunity I had missed in the North, as I realized with regret.

At dinner that night I told Alma I'd seen her house. She looked so expectant that, although my more lasting impression was different, I only said the house was interesting and would be fun to restore.

She had one last warning: "You are going to miss this town. You'll find out."

I did not think I would. I felt sorry for her and she felt sorry for me . . . and within a year she would have moved back to the States and I would be living in Nome, and she would have given up her house and I would be buying it.

The threads of Bobo's new life had been spun by that day. From then on the pattern could start to take shape.

The lemmings were found at Barrow. Not many of them; they were scarce everywhere, even during the following summer. But up at the farthest-north tip of Alaska there were a few, as Arnot Castel had predicted. On the flat, endless tundra behind the town, again with an Eskimo and a shovel, I was digging out lemming burrows without glimpsing a single occupant. Finally, however, late on a dull Sunday afternoon, I returned to the Eskimo home where I was boarding and indoors heard the excited chattering of a dozen children. They were surrounding eleven-year-old Joe Ningeok, who was holding a tin can with one hand across the top. He gave it to me, and I saw that a ball of silky brown fur was huddled down in the bottom.

I put the small creature into the glass and plywood cage I had brought, and watched with almost incredulous wonder this first of my lemmings. His fur was so long that it almost dragged when he walked, and therefore he didn't look anything like a mouse—more like a tiny marmot, with a blunt, upturned nose, ears almost lost in his fur, and a half-inch white tail, fully haired and arched up like a little Husky's. He wagged it from side to side as he examined his new quarters, and he had his say about all of this with a sweet, plaintive chirring.

Spurred by Joe's reward, the children found five more lemmings, catching them in the outside runways in empty tin cans. Six were all they were able to get, although they continued to hunt for the whole month I was there. And one of the six had to be turned loose because he was so belligerent that he endangered the other lemmings. Hoping fervently that this nucleus of a colony would breed, I took the caged lemmings to Nome.

By the time those five lemmings were found, they had in my own mind a very high value for "mice." But the whole price had yet to be paid. I still had to get back to civilization with them, and that wasn't as simple as merely buying an airplane ticket.

Even getting to Barrow had been almost as complicated as getting to St. Lawrence Island—again due to military regulations, in one of those childish ways history has of repeating an impressive performance. By the summer of 1950 the Korean War had broken out and the security situation in Alaska was tighter than ever. The Navy, which had an oil-research program based five miles from Barrow, let it be known that they did not favor trips by civilians up to the Eskimo village. Though they were not actually prohibiting anyone's coming, they made it almost impossible to go by contracting for all the civilian aircraft that had been making the regular run from Fairbanks.

I went up on a charter flight. When we landed at Barrow, the pilot told me to send him a radio message at Fairbanks as soon as my lemmings were found, and he would return. I had the lemmings in less than a week, but the plane in which I had come had run on a riverbar somewhere and was wrecked. And so I found myself stranded at Barrow, living with an Eskimo family who didn't want to put up any traveler for that long, and knowing that the Navy here were no more impressed with my need for lemmings than the officers at Nome had been. They made their disapproval quite clear when we would meet on the village lanes. To make the wait harder, I was not very well, not being able to handle the kind of Eskimo food I was eating here, and I couldn't sleep. The midnight sun at Barrow seems brighter than the sun at noon. It is 'way above the horizon, and in the fine weather of that July it shone with a glare like a blast in the windows of my uncurtained room.

Finally then, on a windy day, a welcome small plane arrived—a Cessna 170, piloted by George Harrington. We were to leave the next morning. Fairbanks, Barrow, and Kotzebue, are the points of an almost perfect equilateral triangle, the distance between each two being about five hundred miles. Since I was taking the lemmings to Nome, which is near Kotzebue, it seemed sensible to fly southwest, direct to Kotzebue, rather than going the long way around, via Fairbanks. There would be no weather station, no airfield or help from the Civil Aeronautics Administration on the route we would follow, but I knew George Harrington's reputation: he was a good pilot and he had flown the route once before. It led for about four hundred miles over the limitless, flat arctic plain, where there is no distinguishing feature, not even a willow bush, to break the monotony of the tundra ponds. No other part of Alaska is thought so unpromising for a search if a plane comes down—but why would our plane come down? In the last hundred miles we would have to lift over a rather high mountain range, and then we would be at Kotzebue.

With the carton of caged lemmings stowed away in the back of the plane, we set out, following the coastline for twenty miles and passing the lonely monument at the spot where Will Rogers and Wiley Post lost their lives. Then we turned inland and began the flight over the thousands of square miles of featureless tundra.

There was an extraordinary amount of smoke in the air—bush-fire smoke, so George told me. The Alaska bush fires burn perpetually in the sphagnum moss, which is seven feet deep in some places and traps so much oxygen that the fire smoulders all through the winter, under the snow. In very dry summers, like that one, the fires can gain headway, and their smoke is like that of a forest fire.

The smoke became thicker. We should be approaching those mountains—and by now we could not even see the ends of the wings of the plane.

"We'll have to turn around," said George. "I don't dare go on. We'll be smashing into a mountainside if we do."

"Have you enough gas to get back to Barrow?" I asked him.

"I don't know," he said, "but we'll have to try it. If we come down, keep your seat belt fastened. We'd nose over, but I think we'd survive the landing." He spoke as casually as if he had said, "Wear your rubbers. It's probably going to rain."

The long, long flight continued. We were facing into the sun now, over that watery plain, everywhere the same. The gas gauge went down and down. I was watching it too, but somehow I wasn't much frightened.

I was more disturbed at the thought of returning, for an indefinite time, to Barrow.

"Why don't you call the Navy," I asked George, "and find out whether they'd take me *away* from Barrow? They wouldn't bring me up but maybe they'd be so glad to have me go that they'd let me ride out to Fairbanks on one of their planes."

George called on his radio and when he had finished the conversation, he turned to me with a grin:

"They say they'll be more than willing to take you out. This afternoon. They will hold a plane."

George didn't try to fly from the airstrip at Barrow to the Navy field five miles farther along the coast; both the gas tanks registered empty. The Navy sent up a tractor with a skid behind it and required me to ride with a coat over my head so that I could not see their research installations.

And now the lemmings and I were installed in a twin-engined C-47, or DC-3 as the plane is known in commercial use. We were the only passengers. This plane too ran into the bush-fire smoke, and it also had to cross mountains, the Brooks Range, but the pilot of course had instruments. He didn't have any instruments that would show clouds, however, and over the mountains we flew into the center of a thunderhead.

The plane tossed like a scrap of paper. And again I thought, Well, mostly it's been a good life—and I did find the lemmings! But an hour later I was walking into the lobby of the Nordale Hotel in Fairbanks. My knees were shaky and I was tired, but I was alive.

And were the lemmings? Had they survived an entire day shut up without air, and an altitude of some 12,000 feet, and the hurling about of their cage as the thunderhead pummeled the plane?

The desk clerk said, "You can just leave that carton down here, as long as you're flying to Nome in the morning."

"Oh, no, I have to take it upstairs," I said. And then, proudly, "That carton contains lemmings!"

"What are lemmings?" he asked.

Voluble, as I always am after a flight that has seemed rather hazardous, I started to give him a little lecture about those important animals: "Lemmings are small, mouselike——"

"Mice! You can't take any mice to your room!"

But I did. At that point I believe I could even have swayed the military. And when I unwrapped the carton and lifted out the cage, and parted the sphagnum moss with which I had filled it to cushion any possible bumps, there, in a close little huddle, were all my lemmings, all living. Within a few minutes they were spinning their activity wheel.

I slept well that night, except for a nightmare or two. And the next morning we flew to Nome.

Tragically the fine pilot, George Harrington, lost his life several months later, as he was flying near Barrow. He was transporting a demented woman, in clear, windless weather, when his plane nose-dived into the ground. It was thought that the woman attacked him. Before setting out she had told a relative that "We never will get to Barrow."

5

The winter in San Francisco had proved how large was the blank the missing lemmings had left in the picture of arctic wildlife. For this project—on which four years were spent eventually—was not merely to list the habits of Northern animals. It was to be a composite narrative of the arctic summer, which draws birds, whales, and fish thousands of miles every year and induces most of the local creatures to wander as if insatiable to experience the brief, lovely season. I wanted the lemmings to furnish the theme, partly because there seemed a poetic analogy between their too-early end and the end of the summer itself in the North, where "the fall of the flowers can be sensed even before they have bloomed." The migration of lemmings would pace the summer.

I had planned to return to the arctic for only as long as necessary to get some lemmings into a cage and myself back onto a plane with them. As their importance grew with the winter, however, I wondered whether the difficulty that other naturalists had had in keeping their lemmings alive could have been due to their taking the little animals out of their own habitat, away from their own kinds of food, water, hours of daylight, barometric pressure, weather, relation to the Magnetic Pole—all the conditions typical of a place in one latitude that would not be found in another. Those conditions may have more influence on animal lives than we know. Once the thought was reached, there seemed only one thing to do: act on it. Therefore I closed my apartment in San Francisco and sent to Nome several cases of books and everything else I would need for a stay of several years.

The prospect of living there for a while was no hardship. Alma was right: Nome did have a curiously long-lasting attraction. At that time I could not define it, but it was only with pleasant anticipation that I landed in Nome with the lemmings.

Within a week I was living in Alma's weather-worn "castle," which was everything that I did not want—rooms too large and too many, too few conveniences, the whole house too dilapidated; it took no imagination to guess the way wind would blow through the cracks. Nevertheless, that was where I found myself. Both of the small hotels had reserved their rooms for the guided parties of tourists who were flying in every day, and the town was crowded—other quarters had all been taken by Army personnel who were building a sea wall that summer.

Remembering Alma, I went around to her house to ask whether she'd rent a room. A truck, loaded with household goods, was backed up to the door. For Alma was leaving her husband, and Nome, and had relinquished the house to its former owner. He was the fire chief, she told me from under an armload of blankets. I went down to his office and rented the house without having seen its interior, and by dinnertime I was living there.

I didn't have any furniture, but a few pieces went with the house—an assortment discarded by previous occupants and looking as if they had been collected here for a rummage sale. They were rather consistent in style, at that: a round oak dining table with claw-and-ball pedestal, a sofa, a broken rocking chair, a china cupboard with glass front and sides (to ship it up from Seattle must have cost more than its original price), a portrait of somebody's pompous ancestor in a plaster frame covered with gold leaf, and an old phonograph cabinet. All would prove useful.

I didn't see the upstairs for two weeks, for the stairway was being remodeled and was impassable. But anyway I'd decided that I would live in two downstairs rooms: the living room, which was long, with white pillars making a semi-division, and the kitchen. The floors were depressing, paint over linoleum—nine layers of it in the living room, as I later found, and twelve in the kitchen. (The Eskimos who were then tearing it up said, "Your floors will be colder now." They weren't, however, because the floors were of solid wood four inches thick.) After the floors were refinished I put down some white caribou skins I had bought from the Unalakleet Eskimos, but the first night I slept between the skins, as the Eskimos do themselves.

It was a noisy house. Even before the sun went down, the place had a midnight feeling to it, with its creakings and shudderings in the various dark alcoves and storerooms that seemed to open from every wall. The loose wallpaper shivered in a strong draft (a large panel of the front door was gone) and moths were skimming around the high ceiling and flapping against it.

I had thought I would be too tired to go out to a restaurant for dinner and had bought some eggs so I could make an omelet. Perhaps they were left from the previous summer, or certainly from the June freighter, three months earlier. I broke eight of the eggs before finding one that was edible. (Two exploded at the first tapping.) I decided I didn't after all want any dinner.

The moment was rather cheerless. To lighten it I put the discarded eggs in a pan and took them out to the blue-eyed Siberian dog, who was lying in front of the house on the boardwalk. He rose, as all cautious animals do when approached, but he didn't come forward. I put the pan down on the walk and he lapped up the eggs while I stooped, to sit on one heel—a good way to inspire animals' confidence, for a human being cannot attack very readily from that position and animals read such meanings.

When Bobo had finished the eggs he continued to stand where he was, looking into my face with the same unwavering gaze I remembered. Would he allow me to put my fingers into the fur under his ear? It is a touch that most dogs accept as friendly. I tried it, but he tossed his head so abruptly that it knocked my hand aside, and he himself turned away. I had been right the earlier time: he would allow a small boy to rumple his coat, lean against him, treat him as freely as puppies would, but he wanted no petting from an adult, no such affront to his dignity. And that was his feeling as long as he lived, however fond he and a human being might become of each other.

He was a dog with a certain and special status, and he tolerated nothing from any creature that would deny it.

Bobo's owners, the family of "Sonny" next door, lived in a house that was built flush with the boardwalk. When Bobo wanted to romp or sleep in somebody's yard, therefore, he came to mine. It was not in itself very inviting, though no worse than the other Nome "lawns," being composed of crushed rock from the tailing piles of the gold dredges. The rock is spread over the ground to keep the permafrost from turning to muck in the summer. A little beach grass was gaining a foothold, but there was no tree, no shade. The only tree in Nome, the only tree within ninety miles, was a wild willow about ten feet tall that my neighbor across the street had transplanted.

That neighbor was Gunnar Kasson, one of the two dog-mushers—Leonhard Seppala was the other—who brought the diphtheria antitoxin 660 miles to Nome during the 1925 epidemic. Their team leaders, Kasson's Balto and Seppala's Togo, quite rightly won as much praise as their masters, for without those two strong-willed and intuitive dogs, the teams never would have got through the dense blizzards. If Balto had still been alive when I moved to Nome, a group of dog subordinates certainly would have gathered under his master's willow. Since he wasn't, the dogs played in my yard, no doubt attracted there by the family dog, Bobo.

From about nine o'clock in the morning, the area under my windows was a boiling of long, fluffy tails—plumes that swung and whirled, quivered aloft in suspense, slowly and gracefully drooped, to be flung up again and whip from side to side with a grand sweeping motion, faster as the dogs became more excited. For these dogs were all Huskies or Husky part-breeds, and playing free, as they were here, their action was brilliant.

Perhaps only in Nome, perhaps nowhere else in the world but that yard, could one have watched Husky dogs enjoying themselves as they wished. Most Huskies are used in teams, and everywhere in the North sled dogs are kept chained to stakes. There were teams in the town; half the Nome population were Eskimos, and those natives used dog sleds to take them out on the sea ice to fish and hunt, to haul fresh ice from rivers for drinking water, to freight supplies to their cabins, and to travel to nearby villages. Then in August there was no snow and the sleds were not used, but the Eskimos' dogs were never turned loose. The Huskies that had the status of "family dogs"—I have not heard them called pets in Nome—belonged to white settlers who had chosen the sled-dog breed as companions.

Those were the dogs that formed the voluntary pack wrestling in front of the house. At some other places and times the fights were in earnest, usually because they involved a female in season. But female dogs were required to be tied up in Nome, and therefore the dogs in my yard were all males.

The play was not noisy, since Huskies can't bark and they don't bay or howl when romping. It was only a rather intense form of exuberance, the Huskies expressing spontaneously the strength that a team would spend in running from forty to fifty (or in the case of a Siberian, sixty-five or more) miles a day.

All of their play was not combat. Much of it simply consisted of frisking around. There was some pressing against each other—much as boys push each other around, and as wolves do, described unforgettably by Adolph Murie in *The Wolves of Mount McKinley*. The wolf pack that Dr. Murie observed for many days and nights had a get-together each evening before starting out to hunt, a frolic of much tail-wagging and sniffing at one another and pushing and "hugging," that Dr. Murie always judged to be friendly. The wolves had young to feed and therefore the play had to end, with the one that would guard the pups going back to the den and the rest trailing off to hunt. But these Huskies were fed by their owners, and while they still showed an urge to find some, at least, of their food, the need was not great and they could continue their romping for a longer time than wolves could.

All of those Huskies had some wolf blood in their strains, and that could have been the source of their high spirits, since adult play is typical also of wild wolves; or their inherited energy could have been due to the fact that Huskies are bred for strength. Even the dogs that were well into middle age, as I later learned, would tumble and bound around in the most lively way. When Bobo himself was ten years old, people who did not know him would smile at the spring in his step and the bouncing tip of his plume and say, "He's just a puppy, isn't he." He was only three, in the prime of his speed and endurance, during those days when I first was watching him.

Only gradually did I realize that any time he was involved in a wrestling match, he was the one standing over the other dog at the finish. He was not the largest but apparently he was the fastest, and he seemed the most versatile—when one could disentangle the lightning moves. Up on his hind feet, he boxed; he attacked from the front; he fought at the side of the other dog, pushing flank to flank as he reached for the other's neck. But of all his manoeuvers, the best was to grasp his opponent's front leg in his teeth and throw him. Some of the part-breed Huskies never had learned that effective trick. It is taught to the Husky pups by their mothers, and those mixed-breed dogs may have had mothers of different lineage.

Most of the full-blooded Huskies had learned it but, fast though they were, they never could seem to defend themselves when the time came that Bobo wanted them on their backs.

Bobo did not always romp. Sometimes he lay on the boardwalk and watched, and then some of the fire was apt to go out of the play. The activity tapered off, and one by one the dogs would lie down to rest—almost as though Bobo himself had kept the activity going and, since he had tired of it, the others welcomed the chance to stop.

Some of them then would sleep for a while, but usually not Bobo. He had an old wound in his right foreleg and, lying there in the sun, he would lick the glistening white hairs above the slight swelling, with his blue eyes preoccupied, as if he knew something he could not share. By that time I was wondering if the thing that he couldn't share was a sense of authority.

When Bobo rested, one other dog always did: Polar, the big white Husky that trailed Bobo so closely when the pack was exploring Front Street. Polar had virtually no life except what he borrowed from Bobo. He seldom sniffed at anything unless Bobo did, never paid any attention to other dogs unless Bobo concerned himself with them. He got up and lay down almost as if he were Bobo's appendage, and this degree of devotion may have been boring, for much of the time Bobo ignored Polar, and the white Husky remained with him just as faithfully.

In his quieter moments Bobo was indeed very aloof. He didn't seem arrogant, only dignified and remote. One of my friends later said, "He has lonely eyes."

He would have been lying with forelegs out straight in

front of him. When he was ready for action again, he rose by unbending his hind legs first, so that his rump was high while his forelegs were still on the walk. In that position he pulled the kinks out of all his muscles. Then, swinging his body forward, he would be up on all feet and starting to trot away down the road. The other dogs fell in behind him at once—and the pack were off for the day's foraging expedition.

Bobo's magnetism, which must have been the influence that drew so many dogs to this yard; his superior fighting ability; the way that the other Huskies timed their actions to his, and waited for his initiative to set out on their explorations—all these seemed to add up to the meaning that Bobo was one of those rare, always interesting animals that are born with the instinct for leadership. There continued to be more evidence. When we had been neighbors for several weeks, Bobo would walk to the post office with me, and in that distance of only three blocks we have collected as many as eight or nine other dogs. They would have been wandering around aimlessly, but when Bobo appeared they moved along with him as if now attached to him with an invisible harness.

And there was one clinching episode, amusing to everyone but the children. During the annual dog-sled races one was scheduled in which family dogs each pulled a child on his sled. Bobo easily outdistanced the others—and sat down to wait until they could catch up. When they did join him, they would not pass him—for by temperament and custom they were his followers! The frustrated youngsters urged and prodded their dogs, but even their little masters didn't have the authority with the Huskies that Bobo had.

This Bobo, then, would be well worth watching. For I already knew that the leadership instinct is of interest to scientists, to psychologists who would like to know what makes a man a natural human leader, and to biologists who are impressed to find leaders among a few species of simpler animals. The instinct is recognized but not well understood, and specialists in the social life of animals, like Professor W. C. Allee, had been asking for "a closer and more revealing study than has appeared as yet of the qualities that make for leadership." I knew that I could not contribute anything of real value, for I couldn't combine a serious study of sled dogs with one of lemmings—not when one species would be ravenous for the other! But I could watch Bobo and in my own mind check his ways with those of the Husky leaders of teams in the Eskimo villages. Already he seemed more significant, because he had assembled his own pack of followers out of the loose family dogs at Nome, and because he ruled them without a driver's help and co-operation. He was more, it seemed to me, like the leaders found in the wolf packs that apparently decide when, where, and how to hunt.

Two or three Eskimo carpenters worked at my house during the early fall, making repairs without which I felt that I could not live in it. The way they watched Bobo outside seemed a kind of tribute to his compelling temperament, and they also talked about him more than one might have expected. One said, "That dog is wolf, maybe five, six grandfathers back."

I asked why he thought so. The natives discussed the question and agreed on several features in which he was "like wolf, more than some Huskies."

They pointed out the very long fur on his shoulders, especially the white ruff, in which the hairs were nearly five inches long. They also spoke of the black "mantle" over his upper back, the rest of his back being gray; the size of his feet, nearly the five-inch length of a wolf's foot; and the form of his face, with its width at the back of the jaws.

All Huskies are indeed wolf-like in appearance. Some of the larger Huskies can't easily be distinguished from wolves. I have at the present time a Husky, named Tunerak, that has as many wolf characteristics as Bobo, but different ones—in Tunerak a wolf's golden eyes, eyes which slant more than Bobo's, more as a wolf's would; and especially Tunerak's tail, which sometimes he carries high but as often swings in other directions, a most limber, expressive tail, with a wolf's bend in it about four inches below the base. To see the tail only, one would assume that Tunerak is a wolf.

Tunerak has large feet, like Bobo's, but almost no ruff or mantle. He has all the traits of temperament that I thought were wolf-like in Bobo—except the leadership. Tunerak would be one of the faithful, co-operative followers that make a wolf pack such a harmonious organization. Whereas only a good strong chain would hold Bobo if it was necessary for him to be confined, I could hold Tunerak with a piece of string. I do tie him up with a slender rope, which he does not chew because I have asked him not to! He is very easy to live with, but he lacks Bobo's great dignity and his startling initiative.

In Nome that September there was an Indian summer after the first hard frost. The weather was so deliciously warm that the front door was open all day, and I sometimes went out and sat on the steps to enjoy the sun. Once Bobo walked over and stood in front of me, and I studied his wild and sensitive face, his eyes even a little more intense than usual, his ears flickering to catch sounds that were inaudible to mine, and his muzzle and nostrils constantly, delicately in motion, in the way that has made William Berry, the wildlife artist, say that he finds wolves very difficult to paint, because their muzzles continually, subtly change shape.

Bobo's eyes were not meeting mine. They were looking into the open door, and one of the Eskimos, who was working near by, weather-stripping a window, said, "I think that dog smell your sky-mice."

The sky-mice, the priceless lemmings!

"No, Bobo—no!" I cried, and jumped up and went inside, closing the door behind me.

6

"Outside dog" was the label given in Nome to any imported pet, and also to any local dog of mixed breed that was not predominantly Husky. In this unconscious way the people acknowledged that Huskies were the right dogs in this Northern town. The laws and police rules concerning dogs gave consideration to the habits of Huskies rather than outside dogs. When the wife of a rather important official moved up to Nome, bringing her cocker spaniel, she was afraid that the Huskies would kill him if he were allowed to run. She wrote a strong letter to the newspaper demanding that all the *large* dogs be kept chained all the time, but no such regulation was made.

Everyone knew that the Eskimos' Husky teams had attacked people occasionally, and when the loose pack of dogs became about team size there was uneasiness. Then the police did require that all dogs be tied up for two or three weeks. The pack would disintegrate somewhat during that period, and the smaller number that reassembled seemed safe.

Most owners of Huskies thought that the reasons why teams might be dangerous did not apply to their family dogs. Probably they were right, but strays also roamed around Nome. Some were hungry, and even the most experienced musher could not predict what they would do. From time to time, therefore, the dog community had a shaking up, and when the Huskies were turned loose again, Bobo's followers might be reduced for a while to three or four.

The outside dogs were themselves a hazard, partly no doubt because they didn't know how to fit into the Husky society of the North. In the most basic ways it was different from the dog relationships the outsiders had known before. And the very size and strength of the Huskies must have been disconcerting—here was a place where the *average* dog weighed between sixty and more than a hundred pounds. How did the pack of Huskies look to a beagle? A dachshund?

Some of the outside dogs, however, refused to accept an inferior status. Two were no more than amusing. Hubba, a little terrier-type, seemed masochistic in the persistent way he harassed the Huskies. They did not kill him, but fairly frequently they gave him the thrashing he seemed to ask for. His mistress, Margaret Mozee, the wife of the U.S. marshal, had been a public-health nurse, and she knew so well how to care for his wounds, and she made him such a comfortable, even pampered, patient that one wondered if Hubba associated his challenging of the Huskies with that special care. Bobo was never one of the dogs that punished Hubba, but there were times when Hubba kept barking around his nose that Bobo would throw me a desperate glance. I took it to mean, I can't stand much more of this—and I would send Hubba home.

Another small dog that seemed to pride himself on his fearlessness was the town character, Nippy. A wirehair-dachshund mix, he was fairly ridiculous in appearance, but he won the respect of all dogs, and men, by the sheer power of a disdainful temperament. Nippy, independently going his way, turned aside for no one. I've never known him to threaten people, but he passed the Huskies with one of the most ferocious growls that could issue from any dog's throat—and continued along the road without even a sidewise glance. Bobo's hair would rise, but he always let Nippy get by with his impudence. Bobo never attacked any smaller dog, whether from pride or conscience no one could say. He had both.

To reject other dogs, and reject them contemptuously, was the special form of aggression used by one of the outside dogs, a large male, Bobo's match in strength, named with exquisite suitability: Spider. The amount of hatred that Bobo and Spider felt for each other was even a little frightening. For whenever they saw each other, no human observer could miss the very great power of both to do harm.

Spider admittedly was a handsome dog, tall, well-built, all silken black except for a white star on his chest and white feet. But he had such an insolent manner that even quite mild and easygoing people would speak of him irritably. They probably would have agreed with Bobo that a miniature like Nippy can be disdainful if that's his pose, but the attitude is intolerable in a dog of threatening size.

Spider walked with the stiffly held head and legs with which one dog approaches another to fight—only Spider did not approach; he walked away, and he could make it seem that he wouldn't fight because the other dog wasn't worth taking seriously. He put down his feet with such prissiness, one would say that he even rejected the ground. He would receive a cookie from a child as if it should have been two cookies, or at least a better cookie—an amazing, unhappy animal.

One day when I stood on the walk on Front Street, talking to the chief of police about Bobo's pack, Spider, alone as usual, came along. As he passed us he gave us a wide berth, stepping out to the edge of the walk. The policeman's eyes followed him with dislike. "We're just waiting until that Spider shows the first sign of snapping at somebody. Then he's going to have a bullet through his head." But Spider gave them no chance. It was my own belief that Bobo was the real object of Spider's venom and that Spider was, in a way, saving his animosity for an eventual showdown.

Spider may have been a more pleasant dog in his puppy-hood; jealousy of the leader, Bobo, may have poisoned his temperament. For Spider, too, undoubtedly was a forceful dog, one that felt he should dominate, and he hadn't a single subordinate. Both the Huskies and outside dogs avoided him—except when he rode in his owner's truck. Then the dogs would vent their dislike of Spider by chasing the truck, barking and howling furiously. They apparently felt that they could express themselves safely while Spider was rolling along, he and they inaccessible to each other.

Bobo would be the dog leading the chase—to his discredit, a human would say, since the performance was so undignified. The pursuers almost, but not quite, could keep up with the driver's speed, and after a block or two the truck drew away from them. Spider would have been looking off over the heads of the dogs, not barking any response, not even seeming to know they were there, but it must have given him satisfaction when they had to give up and pretend sudden interest in something along the road. Bobo always identified the black pickup, which hardly could be distinguished from others in

Nome of its make and age, and he would tear after it—almost as often when Spider was not in it as when he was.

On the ground he and Spider kept well apart. If Spider so much as passed our street at the end of the block, Bobo would stiffen, and Spider, aware of him too, would walk ever more slowly and mincingly, whereupon Bobo would whimper, an anguished inner cry, not a challenge. For half an hour or more Spider might loiter around that corner—not coming down into our block, however—and all the time Bobo would watch him, looking sickened, with his brow furrowed, as all Huskies' foreheads are when they're troubled, and with his mouth grim. No doubt the dogs sensed that they were so nearly equal in strength that one could not hope to defeat the other until he had some unusual, extra advantage . . . and so they waited.

Undoubtedly Spider and Bobo represented the two kinds of domination that psychologists find in animals as in men: despotism and leadership—and the same words are used in regard to animals. Despotism is the more common, by far. In the species where it occurs, tyranny is not only typical of the individuals at the top, but is likely to be a trait of the weaker ones any time that they have a chance to express it. The group organization takes the form of hierarchies, with every creature subservient to the ones above and despotic to those below—an arrangement best known in chickens, where the line of aggression is the much-publicized peck-order.

As all farmers know, a hen despot intimidates every other hen in the flock, by pecking it or eventually only threatening pecks; the second in line assaults all but the top tyrant—on down through as many as twenty-five chickens, each of which knows its place, knows the ones it can peck and the ones before which it must walk with a lowered head and a slower step. (Quickness of motion seems to inflame those of the upper strata.) The hens of high station often have subordinates that they treat indulgently; and amusing too are the frequent "dominance triangles," in which A pecks B, B pecks C, C pecks A, but no hen below them dares to peck any one of the three social rivals. Whatever the favoritism, however, or reluctant sharing of rank, the relationship between members of any despotic social order is not a friendly one, although there is some stability about the group once they get their positions settled. Hens, for example, lay more eggs after they know where they stand with each other.

Such lines of descending tyranny are found among dogs of the sort that have been long domesticated, the dogs in conventional neighborhoods where there may be as many breeds as there are individual animals. Usually the dogs fight it out until they know who can lick whom and afterwards they live in a kind of truce (except when a female in season makes the male dogs lose their heads). The truce is like the uneasy peace among chickens and among the many other species that fall into despotic hierarchies. Those species include some, though not all, birds, fish, insects, and such mammals as mice, ground squirrels, cats, horses, cows, monkeys—and of course, often, men.

The dogs may belong in this grouping—now. Once they probably didn't. There is evidence that the dogs originally had the leader-follower social system.

An animal leader seems to be born with his sense of authority, and with several other traits that will be necessary if he is going to be a real guide to his fellows. Most of the species that produce leaders are among the so-called higher animals, but leaders also occur among a few kinds of ants, lizards, and fish, and even a fish can demonstrate the true leader quality. When one of them has been trained previously to find his way through a maze in a laboratory aquarium, then when other fish are put into the maze with him, he takes responsibility for leading them to the terminal, a route they learn then faster than they do when no leader is there to teach them.

The quality that distinguishes leaders from despots is just that trait shown by the humble fish: a sense of responsibility. As even the cool-headed biologists say, an animal leader "assumes social obligations." The leader will be the one most alert to discover an enemy, and if danger does approach he will make an effort to save the others. Some species that migrate have leaders that choose the route.

In most cases the followers give him their loyalty without discord. Although occasionally he may have to subdue a rival, his group acquiesce to him much more willingly than subordinates do to a despot. The ones that are led also get along better with one another than animals that are ruled. Among followers of an authentic leader there doesn't seem to be the aggressiveness that makes for a line-up of small tyrants under one absolute tyrant.

Wolves are a good example of a successful leader-follower organization. In their kind of hunting an "executive" is needed to co-ordinate the efforts of all the pack, and nature provides those leaders. Some no doubt are better than others, and perhaps at times there would be a surplus of them. One wonders if the "lone wolves"—and they do occur; they are not just a legend—are animals with some talent for leading but without any followers. They would hardly be welcomed into any existing pack by *its* leader.

That the head of a wolf pack is an individual with authority is shown not only when the wolves are running down game, but also around the dens where the wolves have their home life. The rest of the pack are deferential to him even in play. Meanwhile his group of followers live together and hunt in a spirit of the most friendly co-operation. Among them are mated and unmated adults, puppies of perhaps two or three litters and young ones born the previous year. One of the most touching things about the group life of wolves is the way the adults all help to feed and protect the young. Any one of the mated or unmated wolves may bring them meat, and an "aunt" will sometimes stay at home to guard the puppies and let the mother go out on the hunt with the others. Lois Crisler, in her beautiful book, *Arctic Wild*, most of which is about the firsthand experience that she and her husband had with Alaska wolves, tells how an (unmated) pair of wolves adopted five orphan wolf puppies and cared for them with the utmost devotion. There are sex jealousies among wolves (Mrs. Crisler describes an instance) but no infidelity, it appears. Wolves mate for life.

It would not have been possible to visualize the dog Spider in the typical social system of wolves. He showed no signs of a sense of social responsibility, but many of wanting to be a despot. He might have got along very much better in San Francisco, or Boston, or even a farming community, where the other dogs would understand his kind of tyranny. But in Nome the Huskies had the leader-follower system and it must have been baffling to Spider—as Spider's attitude was to Bobo.

And how did dogs, all of which were wolves in their origin, happen to change and become tyrannical with the members of their own species? Perhaps, in the process of domesticating wolves, men bred the spirit of independence out of most of the strains. For men have wanted obedience in their dogs; obedience was required more than any other one trait, they probably thought, if the dogs were to be useful. Eskimos do not want that kind of obedience, but their particular need demands the special qualities of an animal leader. A dog to hunt, however, or to herd sheep, or find lost persons, or just to love and be loved, must "mind," we would say. In reducing his status we have, in a way, humiliated the dog—and is that why he takes it out on his fellows, as the hens, from the beginning despotic by nature, take it out on their humbler companions?

Bobo, so close to his wolf inheritance, did as well as he could in organizing his Husky pack like a pack of wolves. They played together as wolves do, and they apparently had some sense of being united. They co-operated in hunting even though it was only pseudo-hunting around garbage cans and the back doors of restaurants. They were willing to let Bobo's judgment guide them; they waited for him to take the initiative. He defeated any other dog that aspired to be dominant and defeated his own followers when they challenged his status.

But in spite of these relics of the wild days in their lives, Bobo's Huskies had a thin substitute for the wolves' freedom out on the wide, wind-swept tundra. How galling the collars and chains must have been to them, and the attitude of those owners who failed to understand that a Husky is not like other dogs and should be treated as a respected companion, not as a slave. How tantalizing must have been the dog meal in which any meat was disguised as hay, while the Huskies' owners ate meat, and the tormenting smell of meat issued from butcher-shop doors.

Most distressing of all may have been the fact that the Huskies could have no permanent mates and no family life. I used to wonder what inner conflicts the dogs suffered in trying to reconcile their deeply-ingrained instincts with the way male and female Huskies were separated in the human environment. How frustrated did Bobo feel when the wild voice within gave him commands he could not possibly carry out?

It would say:

You have found a companion who is congenial, and she will be your mate. You will stay together for all your lives. A rather large number of wolves never do find that companion—but you, Bobo, are fortunate. You have Tulle, your little neighbor.

You must make a den where you will live together. A litter of puppies will be born to you every year. While Tulle is nursing them, bring her meat to her. Later you both will bring meat to the young ones. As they grow, you and she will teach them to hunt, to defend themselves, to be clean, and to live with the other wolves peaceably. There will be unmated wolves in your pack. They will not try to win Tulle away from you, but they will want to help feed and train your puppies, and don't be jealous, but let them do it.

When other new puppies are born, the older ones still may

*want to stay in your pack. Don't drive them out; if the pack
becomes too large, they will leave and form one of their own.
It's a disadvantage, true, when too many wolves hunt together. Fifty can't bring down many more mountain sheep
or caribou than fifteen can, and the hunting of only one band
of you will not feed fifty wolves. Fifteen makes a good-sized
pack (about the same number that you have gathered together in Nome—but of course those in your pack are all males,
and that is not right).*

*The aim is always to form a pack that will live harmoniously
and be efficient in hunting. But first you must have your own
family, and why do you wait? Tulle is coming in season now.
In about sixty days, then, she should have a litter of puppies.
And in sixty days the cold winter winds, full of sleet and
snow, will be blowing. You must not let them blow on those
helpless young. What kind of wolf are you, Bobo, that you
spend your days playing in the bright autumn sunshine when
you should be digging a den?*

The wild voice would say other things, but then in October
those commands must have been loudest.

Next to my house, on the opposite side from where Bobo
lived, was a vacant lot, and beyond it a log cabin built by a
gold-rush miner. It was one of those little historical cabins
so cherished in Nome: a single room wide and eight rooms
long this one was, the final room being a dog barn, with
collars and harnesses of a gold-rush team of dogs still hanging
on rusty spikes. The weathered wreck of the most beautifully
designed dog sled I've ever seen leaned against the outside
wall.

The original owner had died but the cabin had long been

occupied by another sourdough, a Finn with his dog—every Alaska miner, without exception probably, has a dog. The Finn's dog was Tulle, the prettiest bitch in town and the sweetest, if a human being can judge a dog's preference.

She was Bobo's particular friend. Her owner worked as night watchman in a mining-company warehouse, and he slept during the day. Tulle stayed inside with him while he was getting his supper, but all the rest of the time she was tied outdoors, on a chain long enough so that she and Bobo could play in the vacant lot. Her name, a tender Scandinavian word, means something like "little cuddly thing," and that probably was the meaning too of the name Bobo called her in Husky language. In his flexible voice, he had one particular, poignant, affectionate sound that kept escaping from his throat when he was romping with Tulle. It was a sound that he used at no other time.

Tulle must have had one ancestor that was not Husky, one that had given her golden-brown fur and eyes. The eyes were exquisitely soft and trusting and, whenever she looked at Bobo, adoring. She would brush his face with a nose-touch as reticent as his own, and then so delicately would curl her head under his that Bobo would lose his aloofness and court her with open affection. Standing at full height, looking down at her face with his own eyes like blue electricity, he would stomp a quick tattoo, and Tulle would throw herself down, licking his fur and quivering with delight.

At all times there were expressions of their devotion, and periodically the most ardent love-making. No other Husky ever intruded on that relationship. They stood about in an envious circle but, prompted by their wolf instincts perhaps, they seemed to conclude that Tulle was indeed Bobo's mate.

That was as far as Bobo and Tulle themselves followed their wolf traditions. For some reason Tulle never had bred; there were no puppies that Bobo, even vaguely, might have recognized as his own. But even before the litter would have been due, he never started to dig a den. Of course the soil there was not the right kind, being oozy silt in summer and frozen as hard as granite in winter. They should have had a riverbank or a sun-facing slope to work in. The permafrost at Nome may have been one of the Husky frustrations.

There was no question but that Bobo felt something special about his relationship with Tulle. With its limitations, however, and the artificial situation of many available unmated females at Nome, Bobo did go with his pack whenever the time came that they gathered around one of the other chained bitches. As having top status, too, Bobo expected to have first chance. In those particular circumstances his followers didn't give in without fighting; Bobo came home with bites on his nose and with his ears torn, but usually he had won. Perhaps he *had* to win, since he had his leadership of the dogs to preserve.

Chronically Bobo was listless and a little feverish for a few days. The veterinary at Fairbanks diagnosed his ailment as nervous indigestion. Human beings sometimes assume that nervousness is the result of repressions that civilized family living makes necessary, that they would be healthier if they could live in accordance with "animal instincts."

With Bobo the stress may have been the other way around. His wild nature would have required that he be faithful to Tulle, but there were none of the normal wolf family arrangements at Nome, and to maintain his Husky pack he had to claim for himself the first rights in any prize.

In many ways, but especially that one, it would not be easy to adapt a wolf's instincts to the conditions in a civilized human town.

7

At daybreak on October 10th everyone in our neighborhood woke to a nightmare. The end of sleep, which usually releases us from the more elemental horrors, plunged us into them with a ghastly summons, a din that sounded as if all the dogs in Nome were trying to kill one another.

They were fighting in the vacant lot next to my house. Some were members of Bobo's pack, the others were strays and outside dogs—a yelping, snarling, murderous band, and at the center of it, Bobo and Spider. Eighteen dogs, led by Spider, all were attacking Bobo. Only one, Polar, his friend, was fighting beside him.

The pair could not possibly do more than hold them off; they could not defeat eighteen others. Dogs that would not have dared even to stiffen in Bobo's presence now were dashing in for quick clamps of their jaws in his flesh; they tore at his fur. With a flashing speed Bobo returned their bites. He, and Polar not quite so fast, whirled and spun to fend off the teeth that were snapping from every side.

The Huskies' most frequent attack was to grip a foreleg, attempting to throw Bobo. As he, then, closed his teeth on their ears, they would fling up their heads, trying to reach his throat—and Bobo's own head would go down. He could cope with the Husky methods.

Spider however did not fight as a Husky does. Spider's technique was new: his fangs stabbed for Bobo's eyes. As persistently Bobo dodged, and Spider's bites, so far, had gone into the flesh of his face. It was covered with blood. It seemed as if soon the blood and the swelling must blind him.

Unless the fighting already had gone too far, Bobo could have stopped it by asking for quarter. When a dog—or a wolf—sees that he hasn't a chance to win, usually he will end the combat by offering to the foe his throat or his vulnerable underparts. That is the explanation when one of two battling dogs may suddenly turn the side of its neck to the enemy, or roll over onto its back. But Bobo was not admitting defeat. He didn't want Spider's mercy.

It was easy to guess how the fight had begun. Bobo was spending both nights and days at that time with Tulle. On the previous evening several other dogs had been there. The Huskies were jealous but stood away. The outside dogs came in closer. Standing at Tulle's side, Bobo would growl and the tip of his tail, up over his back, would vibrate with indignation. Since all of those dogs were smaller than he, they backed down on their reckless challenge.

Late in the night Spider must have arrived. Bobo's attentions to Tulle had gone on by then for three or four days. He no longer would be in his best fighting trim. Spider no doubt sensed the advantage that he had been waiting for. Tulle's attraction, too, would have made Spider bold. One can imagine his springing attack on Bobo, the more ferocious because it had been long delayed. The other dogs would have seen their new opportunity. Doubtless they had joined Spider to even the score with Bobo and perhaps gain a chance to reach Tulle themselves.

Some of the men of the neighborhood had got up and now stood on the boardwalk in front of the lot. They were helpless to stop the fight, since the dogs were not harnessed. When a team of sled dogs attack anyone, or start scrapping among themselves, they can sometimes be pulled away by the ropes. The loose mob of dogs would have turned on any man who had gone into their midst and had tried to curb them. Some of the men's own dogs were involved, but they could do nothing.

Little Tulle shrank quivering against the log wall of her master's cabin. He would not return home from his work for two hours or more. Later he told me that he had been somewhat worried about leaving Tulle alone outside. He had foreseen the danger of such a fight, but he had hoped for a litter of puppies sired by Bobo and, knowing Bobo's standing with other dogs, he had thought Bobo could hold them off. And so, surely, he could have if Spider had not incited the rest of them.

Blood was flying. Spurts of it literally were flung into the air as a bitten dog sprang around in an attempt to retaliate. The attackers were fighting each other as well as Bobo. And Bobo himself? It was evident that he now could not see. Probably he was tiring, too. His defense was slower. I could not watch any longer. Weeping, I turned away.

After several moments more all the sounds were stilled, rather suddenly. It was necessary to know what had happened.

All the dogs except Bobo were limping off. The men had

come into the lot. They stood motionless, looking at Bobo, who lay on the pebbles as flatly as if he were only the bloody pelt of a dog. One could not see his face at all, only a chewed mass of flesh.

The men were not talking, but they obviously suspected that Bobo was dead. Their faces, lined darkly by primitive stirrings, now slowly were gentling into regret and pity—but were still angry, too. Most of the men of Nome had a masculine admiration for Bobo, that strong dog, that leader, and it looked as if they were offended, personally, as they saw him now—killed?

The man nearest Bobo touched his boot to a hind paw. The paw and leg twitched up closer to Bobo's belly. He was not dead, then? Sonny's father stooped down and put his hand over Bobo's heart. Saying a word or two to the others, he left, to come back with a square of plywood. The men eased Bobo's limp body onto it, and two of them carried him out of the lot.

All the rest of the dogs were gone. I had not seen Spider leave. A week or so later he was riding around in his master's truck. He did not have any visible wounds. And no dogs were following.

From day to day Bobo lived. When the blood was washed off his coat, it was found that he had many bites but none serious except those on his face. Only half of his face was chewed—the right side. It looked like a double handful of butcher's beef—no eye, no form to the jaw, no skin except shreds that were starting to loosen, preparatory to sloughing off. Within a few hours he had been able to get on his feet. Morning and night he would step out the door for a moment and then go inside again, to lie on a blanket, so Ann, Sonny's mother, told me. She said they were feeding him milk, which he was able to lap. As nearly as they could tell, he could not close his jaws.

She said that her husband insisted that Bobo be shot, but the children were so upset at the prospect that they were waiting until they could take Bobo's loss a little more calmly.

After a week or so Bobo was spending his days on the boardwalk. The fall storms were overdue but were holding off in that year, and though the sun was up now for only a few hours—about ten minutes less every day—when it did shine Bobo lay with his face exposed to it, as if its thin warmth felt good.

Patience is a quality that often seems rather negative: a holding off, a restraining of irritation. In Bobo the stillness with which he suffered seemed more like a healing process, a gradual binding up of his nervous and physical strength. He didn't sleep. Either he lay very quiet, or he worked on his wounds. He would lick his front paw, immaculate white, and then rub it over his face . . . over the surface once or twice, clean the paw with his tongue, give it a fresh moistening with saliva, and again smooth it over the flesh. If he could have reached the wounds with his tongue, that way would have been more efficient, but the substitute method showed instinct's adaptability. The raw flesh seemed to be taking a little more the form of the bones beneath, though a string of it six inches long and the width of a finger hung loose, dangling whenever the dog moved his head.

There was no veterinary at Nome. Dr. Maxwell Kennedy, the dentist, also a dental surgeon, had studied some aspects of animal care as a sideline, and he would treat the dogs when they needed help—not for profit, simply with a humane and generous impulse. While I was in his office one day, he said that he had seen Bobo and asked if I'd tell my neighbors that he would be glad to remove the string of flesh from the Husky's face and do any other repair work he could. When I explained the offer to Ann, she shook her head and said, "I think nature will take care of it." She was part Eskimo, a slight, intelligent woman with a dry manner not characteristic of the Eskimo race, though in speaking of Bobo her voice was all warmth and kindliness. It may have been her Eskimo heritage that led her to trust nature's therapy, and time proved her right.

The sight of Bobo's injuries was unnerving at first. Soon however I began stooping to talk to him, and if his face could show little response, the limber and undamaged plume of his tail replied for him. Its expressiveness was so much more than "wagging" that it deserves a different word. For the plume followed the tone of my voice as an accompanist follows a singer.

The voice now enthusiastic: "It was a grand, brave fight, Bobo! You behaved like a leader!" The tail, aloft, swept widely from side to side. The voice slower, more sympathetic: "Tulle was faithful. She didn't let any other dog come near, all the later days." The tail swung more delicately, in a smaller arc. "Your face must have hurt so much. Does it still? It looks terribly painful." The tail, motionless, drooped to the board-walk. "But some day it WILL be healed! And we'll go for such walks on the tundra next summer! The wind will be blowing over the hills, blowing your fur—you'll bound after the plovers!" The tail made a fine, big, circular exclamation point.

I wouldn't suggest, of course, that Bobo knew all those

words, but a tone of voice can convey much, and no one can be completely sure that the pictures in my mind were not thrown on the screen of Bobo's mind. One can doubt the process, but its impossibility cannot be proved. Anyway, it became fascinating to see how much sensitivity we could work out between voice and plume. Later the give and take was between voice and voice, but in those particular days Bobo was not making sounds.

If his plume ever had shown such a matching between our emotions before, I had not noticed it. It was more likely, I thought, that only now did he really accept my friendliness. And perhaps only at this time because he was lonely.

No dogs came around except Polar. Polar arrived at the usual hour each day and waited and, when Bobo came out, would lie on the walk near him. The dogs didn't play, nor was there a nose-touch of greeting, nor any tangible sign of comradely feeling except when Bobo would shift his position. Every hour or so he would get up and make his usual three turns, the instinctive remnant that many dogs still retain of trampling a bed in grass or leaves. When he would lie down again, each time he was apt to be closer to Polar. When Polar was with him, Bobo was more alert; his spirits would seem to sag a little when Polar left. If he ever had taken this faithful friend for granted, it appeared that now Bobo found it a comfort to have him there.

Almost certainly Polar had saved Bobo's life in the fight. He probably was responsible for whatever small margin there was between Bobo's living and his being mangled beyond recovery. Polar: not very sharp, not a very interesting dog, but with boundless love.

Why had the others deserted their leader? Bobo was not

in any condition to set them in motion. His fires had been banked. But the dogs didn't come at all; had Bobo "turned off" his magnetism, in effect, knowing that now he could not enforce his will? Leaders have to be strong, they have to maintain their dominance.

That is a fact well known to the Eskimos. If a lead dog is demoted to run as one of the team, the morale of the team goes to pieces, and the old leader is scorned. When once he has been their chief, the rest of the dogs refuse to accept him as one of themselves, in a lesser status.

In the teams used for racing, the instinctive relationships seem to be held in abeyance. Several leaders may be used in swing and wheel positions; but the racing groups have been put together for one occasion; they are not teams in the usual sense. When the various native villages each send a team and driver to Fairbanks to compete in the annual sled-dog derby, the driver is the town's choice as their best man, and his team is made up of the outstanding dogs of the whole community, nine to fifteen from perhaps as many owners. The dogs race as if they quite understood the objective, so different from that of a hunting trip, and they adapt themselves to the new, temporary leader-follower roles.

The relationship among dogs in the teams owned by white men for sport is, again, different from that of the native teams. In a white-man's team the influence of the lead dog is not absolute.

The Eskimos' teams, organized like the wolf packs, are uniquely dependent on lead dogs. The same degree of reliance of followers on their leader may have been true of Bobo's pack. When he no longer could guide them, the rest of the Huskies probably felt themselves lost or at least confused.

And guilty because they had attacked him so viciously? None of the former fights around the receptive females had been carried to anything like total defeat for the challenged dog; but Spider probably had not been in those other fights.

No new leader supplanted Bobo. The town Huskies wandered about singly, aimlessly. The pack obviously had fallen apart.

The fight, and Bobo's dreadful wounds, were discussed around Nome, and I picked up information about his earlier life.

He had had a good start. His first weeks were unusually "normal" for a half-wild Husky, in that he had the companionship of both his mother and father. They were owned by a pleasant young couple, without children at that time, who liked and understood dogs. Bobo's sire was also the sire of Bobo's mother, making Bobo a line-bred dog. Such inbreeding is usually not successful if carried far, but in the beginning it tends to "fix" the family traits and if these are good, the first offspring may be superior even to their fine parents. My Husky Tunerak also is line-bred and, although not a leader, he too is above average in build, energy, and astuteness.

When the litter of puppies was broken up, Bobo was given to a sergeant at Marks Air Force Base, an installation a few miles from Nome. At the Base the puppy must at least have been very well fed, for the airmen's pets eat the scraps from the mess, which include at times whole roasts of prime rib beef. When the rotation of troops took the sergeant away, he gave Bobo to an Eskimo girl he had met during his stay at Nome. Her family did not own a team, and, since Eskimos do not often have dogs as house pets, Bobo's relationships there may not have been very happy. It would seem that they weren't, because the family did not buy a license for him, and when the police picked him up eventually, the Eskimos did not care enough for the dog to pay the three-dollar fee that would have prevented his being disposed of.

Meanwhile Bobo had been making some human friends of his own. Two were Sonny, then four years old, and his nine-year-old sister, Edith. They were exceptionally nice children; with a white father and part-Eskimo mother, they had inherited some of the best qualities of both races. They were so fond of Bobo that they persuaded their father to redeem him from the police. In that way they had acquired him.

In his first three years, then, Bobo had had ups and downs, with three rather bad experiences that left lasting scars on the sensitive Husky.

Somewhere he had been beaten for, as Ann told me, he could not see a broom or dust mop, or even a yardstick, without being thrown into fear close to panic.

Another dread concerned water. When Sonny's family were out on a picnic one day, a man who was with them dropped Bobo over a bridge railing into the river below. After that incident Bobo would not even romp on the beach with the children, although later he overcame that particular fear.

In a much greater misfortune he had been shot. A town like Nome, so remote and so tolerant, has attracted a few rather extreme human neurotics. One at that time was a man who owned a mongrel bitch. When she was in heat, he would sit in his doorway and shoot the male dogs that came to her. Some were killed; Bobo was only wounded. For the rest of his life however he carried buckshot in his foreleg and hip. In damp weather the leg would swell, and when Bobo was resting he often would lick the leg, stroking, stroking it endlessly with his tongue, no doubt trying to make a pain go away.

In considering what had molded his temperament, one could remember also that he was deserted three times: by the group into which he was born, by the sergeant, and by the Eskimo girl to whom he was given. With a background like that some dogs would have become nervous, wild, and unfriendly. The effect was the opposite in that puppy born with the instinct for leadership. Did he feel homeless in one situation? He found for himself another family to take him in. Had he been frightened by beatings and water and guns? If he couldn't trust people, he at least could have confidence in himself—so much that all other Nome Huskies recognized his authority. It is not necessary to attribute human qualities to the dog in order to recognize what he had accomplished.

How he would react eventually to his defeat and the loss of his leadership was a question that would tantalize any naturalist. But it was one that might never be answered, it now appeared.

By early October the last cranes, geese, and swans had left the arctic. We had heard their voices come down from the sky and draw away towards the south: summer's farewell. We had stood on the boardwalks and listened until the warbling and honking had grown so faint that we knew them for only the pulse in our ears. Bobo's ears turned to the sound for a few moments longer; and then he would start again to rub his paw over his face.

On one of the later days a bowl of clouds, slate-blue, was inverted over that coast. The clouds lifted just enough to show a rim of infinite, incandescent light circling the darkened land. Wanting to see that sky for a little longer, I was outside the house when Ann arrived home from a shopping trip. Before she went in she looked down at Bobo and said,

"We have decided to move to California, anyway for a few years. My husband's mother is sick and he wants to be with her. We're not going to take Bobo, and of course nobody else would have him now. The police will put him away for us after we leave."

"When will that be?"

"The twentieth of November. About a month."

Bobo was three and a half years old—not quite a third of the normal span for a Husky, but in that time he had become a dog that would be remembered a long time in Nome. An animal of extraordinary significance: it seemed unbelievable, as well as unjust and sad, that he could live only another month.

8

The lemmings proved every day that anyone who hopes to learn very much about the way animals live in their wild environment also needs to keep them for a while as captives if possible. Out in the woods and fields everything happens so fast, and what one observer may see is so chancy, that many small, fascinating details are missed.

On the vast expanse of the tundra, for example, how could I have watched the following encounter between two of the six-inch creatures? In the beginning, incidentally, I called each lemming by the Eskimo name of the child who found it, though the names were reduced to numbers for the long pull of the note-taking. I was still at Barrow when I wrote in the daily record of the lemmings' activities:

Alliak, the first lemming found, was given a separate box yesterday. Today I put Eklasook, the one with the bright, red-brown fur, with him. The two ran to each other and caressed with their soft cushiony noses. Then one nuzzled the side and flank of the other. I was gone for an hour. When I came back, Eklasook was asleep under the edge of some grass in the box. Alliak was sitting up, grooming his fur. He would lick his forepaws and, reaching back, brush the fur on his shoulders and head all forward, so that it stood on end and made his head look like a tiny lion's. When the grooming was finished, he ran to Eklasook. They cuddled close and both slept. After a while Eklasook left him and had a meal of grass and moss for herself. Soon she returned to Alliak. A pair?

At Nome that year was a cabinet-maker who once had been a biologist. He constructed the permanent quarters for my small lemming colony: a glass-sided box about four feet long and eighteen inches wide, with a plywood end to which was attached the activity wheel I had brought from San Francisco. The cage, or vivarium, rested on a stand made low enough so that the lemmings would be at eye-level when I was reading or typing. I could look up from time to time and watch their activities at close range.

Into the cage we put a base of several inches of soil, a quantity of dried grass, moss, and other "hay" from the tundra, and small pieces of driftwood, which lemmings nibble, no doubt for the salt, and on which they endlessly run and climb. Other things, such as wood shavings and some foods like raw potato and oatmeal, were added later, but first there were only the simple elements of the natural habitat of the lemmings.

One quite artificial piece of equipment was attached to the top of the cage: a corked bottle of drinking water, suspended upside down with a glass tube that led below to the lemmings' level. The tube was just large enough so that the surface tension of the water prevented its flowing out, but a lemming could get a drink by sucking the tube, or with patience by licking the open end.

At the suggestion of the ex-biologist I stored in an upstairs room a quantity of the natural materials for the winter months when they would not be available: several barrelfuls of dried grass, a stock of driftwood sticks, and, on a boxed-in platform, a cubic yard of earth. My helpers in acquiring these were several small Eskimos, especially the gentle six-year-old, Sonny. One of the pleasures in studying captive animals is the reaction of local children, whose interest in everything about animals is always intense and spontaneous.

The vivarium had no more than been set up and the lemmings installed in it than Eklasook produced the hoped-for increase in the colony:

July 31: For several days (in the old cage) Eklasook has been so quiet that I've wondered if she were sick. She would make a little "form" for herself on top of the grass in the cage and lie in it, eyes looking sleepy and very plump bulges spreading out from her sides. I hoped she was pregnant and assumed that she was when, as soon as I put her into the new cage, she began making a nest with frenzied urgency. She was extremely irritable, attacking the other lemmings and seeming half mad with tension. I moved her back into the old cage and gave her some shavings and cotton. Quickly she dug out a new burrow in the earth at the bottom of the cage and was carrying mouthfuls of the nest materials into it. To watch her work one would say she had only minutes to finish the job. Then she disappeared. By the next morning there were tiny squeaks from her cage. They continued all day.

Infant lemmings must be among the earth's most appealing creatures. When only an inch long they are fully furred and proportioned like the adults, not all legs and heads, as kittens, puppies, and many other newborn animals are. Eklasook had had eight, the same number as her teats and a maximum litter. At the age of two weeks:

The young are finding some of their own food, although they are still nursing. Once while Ekla was feeding herself on some grass a young one was taking her milk. When she was startled and ran for a burrow, he hung on and was pulled along. . . . The small ones are tremendously busy digging burrows and every night rearranging them. They are also great climbers. They are forever running up the wire mesh (on the front of the old cage), working their way across the top, scrambling part way down and, turning their heads to look below, they drop. . . . They have many little peaceful encounters, the mild wrestling, nose to nose, typical of the adults, and also the affectionate nose-touch of greeting. They all return to their mother frequently for that reassurance. But one fought his mother, using his forepaws. As an experiment I put two of the young in the cage of adults. They nosed up to the large lemmings in what seemed an aggressive way but the adults treated them well.

After a few more days I tried moving all the young and their mother into the large cage, but that arrangement had to be changed with haste. The mother was so alarmed for her brood (if that was in fact the reason) that she attacked every other adult lemming—and in those moments was born a plan that worked out quite well. I took the mother and her eight upstairs to the room where the lemming materials were stored, and let them live there as a supply of replacements for the cage, if more lemmings should ever be needed. One of the barrels of grass, tipped on its side, gave the nine lemmings both food and nesting materials; they made burrows in the big box of earth, and eventually I got them, also, an activity wheel. A metal strip a foot wide fastened across the bottom of the doorway would prevent the lemmings' escaping when I opened the door—or so I expected. It remained only to keep them supplied with water. Since there was linoleum on the floor, nothing permanent was damaged or even much soiled. Lemmings have what biologists call the "lavatory habit" of putting their droppings in one place (from which they can be removed easily); and therefore my little zoo functioned to everyone's satisfaction.

It is necessary of course to distinguish between an animal's actions that would be changed by captivity and those that would be about normal even inside a cage. When running in the wire wheel that turned on ball-bearings, the lemmings certainly made better time than they would when running through grass, and perhaps they ran farther per day; but the ways they would wash their fur and do dozens of other small, instinctive things probably would be similar any place where they were. At least one could assume so if all the lemmings went through the same rituals, as they did, although with variations that were impressive.

It is these little, intimate doings that seem to me most revealing. The habits that characterize lemmings in contrast to mice, and even the actions that are different in brown lemmings and those that turn white in the winter: these can inspire as much wonder as man's efforts to reach the moon. For here, in the daily routine of some of the simplest creatures, we are face to face squarely with *life*—not life thought of mechanically, like that of a chicken heart kept beating for months in a test tube, not even life in a laboratory where an animal often is restricted artificially to expressing only one very limited reaction. Those studies of course are important—if they do not lead (as they sometimes do) to an attitude that living beings are no more than mysteriously activated computing machines.

Such laboratory studies, however, leave out the intricate adjustment that each group of animals makes to its corner of the earth; they omit the animals' reaching out for experience and the whole range of their emotions—emotions not being, for some reason, considered significant. A field worker's sense of the marvelous grows as he sees the responses of the natural animal "when he is up and doing," as Dr. William H. Thorpe has written in his absorbing book, *Learning and Instinct in Animals.* The indoor scientists seem too much concerned with putting life into pigeonholes (not the kinds used by birds); whereas the field people think it worthwhile to know how, even in lowly species, one individual may differ from all the others. The feisty lemming that had to be turned loose at Barrow seemed amazingly unlike Mama-neeng, who never outgrew his need for affection—in *lemmings* such variation! It is important, of course, for biologists to know that the Barrow lemmings eat virtually everything that grows in their habitat—including the soil surrounding the grass roots—but is it not also interesting to see that:

Unalean has chewed the clump of muddy roots into an almost perfect cone. He yanks away at the mass of fibers vigorously, and when he gets hold of the base of a stem, he pulls the whole grass blade down through. He eats the seed heads and then he may do one of three things with the rest of the stem. Sometimes he leaves it, parallel with others, at the back of the cage. Or cutting it into short lengths, about three-fourths inch, he takes a number of these in his mouth, crosswise, and runs into his burrow to add them to the walls of his nest. Or grasping the stem, always at the root end, he runs into the burrow dragging the stem and does the cutting while he is in the nest. It seems smart of him to pull the stem by the root end. If pulled from the other end, the branching spikelets would catch in the burrow. With variations all the lemmings utilize grass in these ways. And sometimes they eat all of a stalk, guiding it into their mouths with one forepaw. It disappears steadily and fast.

Of the original five lemmings only one, Mama-neeng, the "adolescent," discovered how to drink from the water tube—until Eklasook bore her young. All her infants caught onto the trick as soon as they were put in the big cage, and during one interlude there their mother learned from them. But none of the other adults: they would put their mouths down against the surface of a dish of water, left on the floor of the cage, and lap it up in what seemed large quantities. In their outdoor environment there is water almost everywhere on the tundra all through the summer, and lemmings apparently find it congenial. They swim very well. As I recorded:

I put one of the lemmings into a tub of water. He swam *fast*, with his shoulders higher than his rump and even most of the rump above the surface, so that he looked as if he were dog-paddling, with his hind feet being the ones that propelled him.

Since the lemmings are creatures that live in the arctic, it seems natural that nests have an absorbing interest for them. They are forever making them, tearing them down, and moving them. The ones they made at the end of their earthen burrows, the little chambers lined with short grass "sticks," would conform to their summer homes. (When they burrow they push ahead with their noses probing into the soil with an up-and-down thrust. Meanwhile their forepaws reach ahead under their chins and push back the loosened earth.) Corresponding to winter nests were their exposed balls of grass fibers, or of cotton or shavings when I put them in the cage. On the tundra these ball nests would be constructed on top of the ground but down in depressions, between the mounds, the frost-boils. It has been found that although the air temperature may be 35° below zero, the surface of the ground under three feet of snow may be as warm as 27° above zero: 62° warmer. The brown lemmings probably don't have to cope with cold much more severe than that down in their

Bobo, Siberian Husky, born with the leadership instinct inherited by a few sled dogs from leaders of wild-wolf packs.

This litter of wolf pups, found by a Barrow Eskimo, probably will be mated with Huskies to sharpen the dogs' instincts.

The face of true wildness: Kim, a full-blooded Alaska wolf.

Husky dogs cannot always be distinguished from wild wolves like these.

Kim's puppies were sired by the Eskimo sled dog Smokey.

Smokey helped rear his young, as wolf fathers always do.

Husky pups with the masks typical of the Malemutes.

Tunerak combines Malemute and Siberian strains with some undiluted wolf traits.

Dogs and people compete for the use of Front Street at Nome.

Eight feet high on a snowdrift, Bobo guarding his gold-rush "kennel."

One of the lemmings that tested Bobo's self-discipline.

Bobo's expressive blue eyes could make his disapproval felt sharply.

Recuperating from battle wounds, Bobo watched for his enemies.

Bobo often brought home neighborhood puppies to teach and to play with.

ditches—over which snow would drift. The white lemmings climb out of the snow for the bark on exposed bushes, and since these lemmings often are found frozen to death, the brown ones (like those I was keeping) seem to have made the more practical adjustment to Northern winters.

One day, to see what the lemmings would do, I gently lifted one of those exposed nests from one end of the cage to the other. By the following morning the nest, all taken apart and rebuilt, had been moved back to its original place.

Usually the lemmings, alert, active, eager little beings, kept very busy. But work wasn't their only interest. They fought for the use of the activity wheel all through the night and sometimes all through the day. Their skill varied, but in each of the lemmings it seemed astonishing. The wheel, like a wire-mesh drum, had a circumference of fifty inches. From the beginning the lemmings' speed was surprising: one revolution, or fifty inches of running, per second. Later this was increased to seventy-five inches. Since the wheel was metered, it also was possible to know how far they ran per day per lemming. The distance at first was nine miles, but that increased until one lemming, alone in the cage at the time, ran 17.66 miles in a twenty-four hour period.

Mama-neeng ran the wheel from the first week with a delightful rhythm. While the wheel continued to spin at a fast, even speed, he would alter his own pace, going ahead more rapidly until he was running halfway up the forward side and then slowing down until he was on the other side— back and forth, a rocking motion very regular and attractive to watch. None of the other lemmings did that, although two had an interesting little game in the use of the wheel:

The lemmings enter the wheel from a hole in the end of the cage, a hole about four inches above the bottom of the wheel and a similar distance from the earth in the cage. While lemming No. 1 is spinning the wheel, No. 2 drops into it and races ahead until he is in front of No. 1. At once No. 1 leaves, without slowing the wheel, and No. 2 continues its speed unbroken. No. 1 returns to the cage, whirls around, goes back into the wheel. No. 2 leaves, again with no interruption in the momentum. He makes the same right-about-face inside, and comes back for another turn. I have seen the two lemmings shift their stints in the wheel eighteen times without any pause. Only these two play the game—and only when the cage is standing in front of one particular window!

Sometimes, not often, two lemmings stayed in the wheel and ran it together. And amusing to watch were the controversies when one wanted to run it clockwise and the other counter-clockwise. If the lemmings had about equal strength, their efforts were like a tug of war and the wheel wouldn't move. If one had more push, the other lemming was carried backwards and eventually had to leave.

I had had the same wheel, attached to the old cage, at Unalakleet, where some mice, tundra voles, had used it. Only one of them ever ran it consistently, and he not as fast or as skillfully as the lemmings. The mice never contested for it, or worked out any games or variations. In other ways too, the lemmings had more fire, more drive—and more impatience— than mice.

The lemmings had many encounters, often affectionate, sometimes belligerent:

Mama-neeng, the small one, met Alliak on a trail. The noses of the two came together with a fiery sputtering. The youngster turned away and Alliak pursued him, nose close to his flanks.

Mama-neeng whirled with a shrill chirring into the big male's face. The big one retreated.

The nose-touch can express several emotions for the lemmings. The noses, being large and round, furnish good pushing surfaces. They will come together tight, a position the lemmings may hold for several seconds, and then both heads go up, with the noses still gripping. These seem to be shoving contests. No sounds accompany them and the lemmings do not seem angry.

When they want a real fight, two approach each other and stop approximately an inch apart, spitting threats with shrill, high whistles. At this stage they may bare their teeth like little ferocious dogs. Then there is a tense, silent wait, each seeming to hold the other motionless with his eyes. One attacks, finally, darting at the other's nose with his nose. The noses grip and both push, a weaving from side to side accompanied by an explosive chirring. In the end one lemming gives up and goes away, usually into the activity wheel to work off his excess emotion.

But there also are many nose-touchings, soft and brief, that seem only greetings. Mama-neeng appeals to the others for it constantly. And when I put something into the cage, he runs up even for me to touch his nose with my finger. As soon as he has this little caress, he turns back to what he was doing. Later he sometimes climbed into my hand and I would hold him for a while, although I was trying not to "tame" the lemmings more than necessary, hoping to be able to watch nearly natural reactions in them.

By late October, when I had had the lemmings for three or four months, all these lemming characteristics and others had been revealed. I thought there were clues as to why lemmings migrate, but nothing more by that time than the faintest suggestions. Even those actions that seemed most significant would have to be checked over a much longer period. However enough had happened so that the project seemed well worth while, even though my personal living conditions grew worse with each passing week.

The autumn storms had begun, the crashing violence of the world's worst weather. The ocean would have congealed by then if the winds had not kept it churned up, for the temperatures were down nearly to zero, but the sea still was flinging its spray aloft. It seemed nearly as sharp as sleet when, with coats slapping about us, we ventured outdoors. My windows, two blocks from the beach, had become opaque with salt.

The house, at that period, seemed a disaster. The winds that entered through cracks in the walls, around doors and windows, and came up through the plumbing, were at times strong enough to lift my hair when I stood in the living room.

The moan of the wind was even more of a trial than its impact. The house had been built in the form of a cross, a design so impractical in the arctic that probably none but a prosperous bridegroom, wanting to give his new wife all the sunlight he could, would have considered it. The couple stayed less than ten years in their Nome house, and subsequent occupants had had to heat all those superfluous outside walls. And had the others been made as depressed as I was by the way the four angles between the walls trapped the winds, which spun around in them, endlessly moaning? Apparently wind got into the little tower, too, and prowled about there, such weird cries came down from that useless turret.

For a few nights—most of the daytime, also, was dark now—I was afraid that the house was haunted. Then I wished that it would be. The empty rooms would have seemed more sociable if I could think that some ghosts were sharing them with me. And there *were* the most eerie sighs and often continuous tappings, on quiet as well as windy nights, during all the five years that I lived in the house.

Whatever the possibility of some unseen tenants, the atmosphere was not gay. The other houses of Nome, clustered closely together, looked friendly and warm with the lights from their windows streaming out on the wintry scene. And some of their owners were cordial, though as yet we hadn't had time to become more than acquaintances. To a few of them I had described my project, and their interest seemed sympathetic.

Startling, then, was a remark made one night at the North Pole Bakery, where I was having dinner. At the long "family-style" tables it was the custom to talk to others, and the conversations had always been amiable until, on this evening, a grizzled character turned to me with a hostile look and said, "Are you the woman that raises rats and has them running all over the house?"

"I'm a naturalist. Right now I am studying lemmings, but they don't run all over the house."

He turned away with no answer, not even in his expression.

In the inevitable gossip about a new resident in a small town, when, where, and by whom had the lemmings been turned into "rats running all over the house"? Every Northerner knows about lemmings. For what reason except animosity would the facts have been so distorted? Walking home in the autumn cold that night, I was more aware of the closed doors than the lighted windows. As I entered my own house, two of the lemmings were spinning their wheel, but when I came near, they ran into hiding. And then all was still, except for the wind, and the rooms seemed larger, darker, and draftier than before.

That dog: yes, that Bobo. I sat down in the mended rocking chair, tilting back and forth as I took a long look at a certainty which instead kept turning into a question.

The certainty: that I could not possibly have a dog living in the same house with the caged lemmings. Any arrangement that placed the lemmings where I could watch them would also make them available to a dog—at least a Husky. And a Husky would be the only kind of dog I would want. It's an attitude that one quickly absorbs in the arctic.

It was Bobo of course that I wished I could take. In the pauses between the storms he still lay on the walk and I still stopped to talk to him—now feeling uncomfortable, however. For didn't I like the dog, and respect him, and wasn't I the one person, probably, who could save his life? Up to that night of the unkind remark in the restaurant, I had been thinking of Bobo in terms of his need, his right to live, and of the interest that a Husky leader would have for a naturalist. So at least I'd have said. Now I knew that I needed his company.

The question: could a solution so right for both of us be denied?

In the morning I went next door. Ann was at home alone. I told her, "Now that I've lived in my house for a while, I find it a little lonely. I would love to have Bobo if you have decided definitely that you aren't going to take him outside. Would you sell him to me?"

"If you wanted him we would give him to you. But are you sure that you want him, with his eye all chewed up like that?"

"I don't mind the eye. I should explain, though, that there is one difficulty. I have some caged lemmings, and I have to keep them alive because they are the reason why I am here—to study them. Do you think Bobo'd attack them?"

"On a trail he would."

"Maybe not in a house?"

"We could try him. We'd all be so glad if you wanted to take him!"

They had no leash for him, since he never walked on a leash, but we tied a rope onto his collar and together Ann and I led the dog in my door. Both of us held the rope, and sensing Bobo's eagerness when he smelled the lemmings, and his strength as he pulled at the rope, I was alarmed even before he had seen the cage.

The lemmings apparently didn't perceive the danger from Bobo's scent. They were particularly conspicuous that day— running about and chirring. When we entered the room and Bobo could see them behind the glass, he nearly went mad with excitement. While Ann and I gripped the rope, and with my other hand I held Bobo's collar, he reared on his hind feet and tried to jump for the cage. How easily one lunge would have tipped it over! It had no top; and even if the glass did not break, as it surely would, all the lemmings would escape, and in my mind's eye I could see Bobo leaping about and catching them.

"No, Bobo, not for you," I said in what I hoped was a soothing but forceful tone. He did not even hear me. He heard nothing, saw nothing, except the little brown creatures darting about on their trails.

Ann spoke with evident disappointment: "It would not work. It would be expecting too much of him."

I said, "Before I decide, let me wait a day or two. I might think of some way to have him, though right now it doesn't seem very promising." But I already knew. I could not have the dog—how could I? With difficulty we led Bobo out of the house. It was a sad day for all of us It was one of the days when I wished for the company of a ghost.

9

The impossibility of my having Bobo was so evident that I went in to tell Ann on the following afternoon.

The day was suitable for so gloomy a mission. A rain, late for the season, had turned to slush, which was coming down out of the sky in handfuls and plashing onto the boardwalk.

Ann was at home. We stood in her sun porch, among all her potted plants and the scraps of a skirt that was on the sewing machine. Behind the sun porch was the living room and past that the kitchen, where Bobo, beyond two open doors, lay in front of the warm fluttering of the fire in the cookstove. His chin had been down on his forepaws when I entered. As I spoke his head lifted up.

"I guess you know what I am going to say. I haven't been able to think of any way I could have Bobo. I do have to keep the lemmings and they have to be downstairs where I can watch them while I am working."

At those words Bobo rose. He walked towards the sun porch with his face turned up to mine, and if now his wounded gaze could not be compelling, in some other way just as effective he was projecting his need. He stopped about four feet away and stood motionless; even the tip of his tail did not sway. The tension was gripping all of us.

Swiftly, suddenly then his self-confidence melted. Rushing forward, he shrank tight against me as terrified children will. I have seen him do that but one other time in his life—during a midnight fire when a blizzard was ripping off sheets of flame from the burning buildings and, with all the town threatened, Nome was close to a state of panic. As a last resort the proud dog would appeal for protection, and the day that his life depended on my decision, he sensed the emergency.

I said, "I don't know how Bobo understands all this, but now, somehow, I'll have to take him."

Ann smiled as if for her, too, an essential right way had opened. That it did would not seem a miracle to an Eskimo, and she would not be amazed at the evidence of a dog's intuition.

The next weeks were singularly contented. I still had no idea how I was going to combine my incompatible animals, but I had confidence that a solution somehow would be found. Actually, though a naturalist, I knew very little about the dog species. As a child I had had a few dogs, but all of their lives came to rapid and tragic ends. One "dog" had been a coyote, a gift to my father as he was making a trip through Texas. In Kansas City the coyote was chained on a wire between trees, but he proved as adept as a locksmith in getting himself off the chain. He'd roam along Warwick Boulevard, calling out to his litter-mates down in Texas. Children were snatched back into their homes by terrified mothers; the police were called. Time after time they went out and recovered the small wolf, and finally they issued the edict that the coyote would have to go. We donated him to the zoo—a not-very-happy outcome to my first relationship with the wild-wolf breed, but it had been an inspiring glimpse of nature untamed, and may have helped to prepare me for the career of a field biologist later.

Even before I had lemmings, it had seemed impossible to combine that career with the ownership of a dog, though a dog would have been welcome company in the various wilderness cabins where I had lived. It had been my ambition to watch the wild creatures over long periods, and describe them for others who did not have that opportunity. That could not be done unless the animals could be seen at close range, acting normally. A dog barking at squirrels, chasing deer, bounding after the chipmunks, would have ended the possibility. I therefore had crossed the company of a dog off my list of longings.

And now I owned one. There was suspense in wondering how the problem would work itself out.

Bobo's wounds had begun to heal faster. As if he knew that his future had been assured—that he had an incentive to live—the flesh pulled together and tightened up, the long string of it sloughed away, new fur started to grow, the swelling drew back in the eye socket. Finally there came a morning when I stooped to greet Bobo and found that an eyeball was partly visible. A new eye had not generated, I was sure, but the state of the old one showed that, even though teeth had gone into it, it was mending. It was brown now instead of blue, but Dr. Kennedy said that probably the brown color was due to blood not yet absorbed. He guessed that the eye eventually would be blue again, as it was. For a long time a slit remained from the eye back almost to Bobo's ear, but even that gap drew together. I tested the wounded eye; with

Bobo's good eye covered, the damaged one followed my hand as I moved it. At least some of its vision remained—and in time might be quite restored.

My dog was then, after all, to be perfect, or nearly so. Actually I had not been disturbed by the thought of owning a half-blind dog. For I'd learned to distrust perfection. As a child I had been obsessed with the wish to have everything "just exactly right." In schoolwork, piano practice, clothes, friendships, I was always making what seems now a frantic effort. No doubt some psychiatrist could say why but, in any case, the years tempered that tendency. For I found that perfection seems to contain an explosive element. It is the ideal living arrangement that proves, for some unexpected reason like a demented neighbor, to be impractical; it is the most understanding friend who moves away; the most treasured souvenir that is lost; the most flattering hat that is blown off and under the wheels of a truck. And if there is going to be a typographical error in the published words, it will be in the paragraph that gave the most satisfaction. By the time that I moved to Nome, I felt that perfection is something to fear, and Bobo had seemed fairly perfect until he was wounded. And now perfect again, since the eye was so thoroughly healing! If perfection it had to be, I would try to cope with it—but I needn't have worried. The explosive element still was functioning.

There was another unexpected but on the whole happy development during those days: I bought that fantastic house. I had employed a white carpenter to build cabinets and the frame for a Japanese bathtub, and at the end of a week's work, when I made out a check for him—$280—it occurred to me that I was putting too much money into a house that was only rented. After the man left I added up what had been spent so far on materials and labor, and the total was well over a thousand dollars. The owner had only been willing to rent the house to somebody who would take it in the condition it was. He made the rent low, but not low enough to justify my financing all the repairs that had seemed essential. Into my mind sprang the thought that I could buy the house, improve it still more, and, with quarters so hard to find in Nome, some day could sell it at a rather good profit. Anyway, for the time I would like to consider the question, I would ask the owner, the fire chief, if he'd give me an option to buy it.

The carpenter hadn't been gone half an hour when I set out to do marketing and stopped at the fire station. The chief was quite willing to sign an informal letter agreeing to a thirty-day option, and at the low price I proposed for the house. He had wished to get rid of it.

Two days later I met him, and he stopped me and said, "Funny thing—fifteen minutes after you left the other day somebody else came and wanted to buy the house. He would have made a down payment right then. It wasn't much but I guess I'd have taken it if I hadn't already signed your letter."

A dark thought: "How much did the man offer you?"

"I forget—two-fifty, two-seventy-five, some odd amount."

"Two hundred and eighty dollars?"

"That was it."

I asked if the carpenter were the man. He was. With my check, paid him for making repairs on my house, he had tried to buy it away from me. Probably he still would if I didn't take up the option. And I'd have to move again—where?

"You don't need to worry," I told the fireman. "I've decided I want the house."

Coming back that night, through the door that didn't fit tight, into the windy rooms, coming back to the stoves that smoked and the wallpaper that bulged, and the half-finished bathroom that now I would have to find someone else to complete—I was pleased, in a deep, quiet way, that this house would be mine. In the proportions of rooms, high ceilings, the fine woodwork, and many windows, the interior of the house was beautiful—though the house had been much abused, almost wrecked, by the combination of arctic weather and careless occupants.

I would restore it! I would bring back to life its original gold-rush atmosphere. Collecting furniture of the period, I would combine the relics in uncluttered modern ways. The house could become an amusing, but comfortable, re-creation of lusty, courageous times.

Such a program would mean that I'd have to stay in the arctic indefinitely. But that plan seemed practical. When the book about Northern animals was completed, I hoped to write one about Eskimos, and I needed to see much more of them. There had been some rebuffs at Nome, but they were effaced by the fact that a bush pilot, who published a little bi-weekly newspaper written by Eskimos for Eskimos, had asked me to spend every other week end helping to edit it. That work would contribute to my own forthcoming Eskimo project.

And Bobo was really the one who made all this possible. Without owning the house, I would not want to stay, and without a non-talking but friendly companion such as that dog, I would not want to live in it. The weeks while I waited for him to move in were one of those glowing times when the future looks only productive and warm and colorful

Ann and her family left Nome on a plane about noon. Bobo was gone somewhere when the taxi carried away the family. I watched for him during the afternoon. I wanted to ease the shock when he found that his door was locked, that he was deserted again, that his people were gone.

The solution to our lemming problem had presented itself a day or two earlier: I would chain Bobo inside the house any time that he was at home. The chain was ready, ten feet of it attached to the handle of the flour bin in the kitchen. The chain would allow Bobo to come into the studio end of the living room, where I worked, and where he could lie on the skin of a blond glacier bear I had bought from an Eskimo for him. There he could feel my companionship, be close to the couch where I slept if at night he were lonely—but could never go nearer than five or six feet from the cage of lemmings.

I did rather dread his first introduction to this arrangement. Would he leap for the cage? And be angry when he could not reach it? Could he break the front off the flour bin? Would the lemmings arouse his ferocity and, if so, how would it show itself? When the lights were out in the night and I could not watch the dog, what would happen? These were misgivings, but I was most concerned to find Bobo and welcome him.

He scratched on my door at dusk—the first time he ever had done that. It was the front door, and I had to let him in the back way to avoid passing the lemmings. From the back door I called to him, and as he entered the kitchen I snapped the chain onto his collar.

I went to the cupboard to get a can of dog food, meanwhile talking to Bobo, trying to make my voice cordial. But when I turned around, the dog's face was startling. He had not moved from the spot where I fastened the chain, and he was looking at me with such anger, such an expression of outrage, that the cheery words failed in my throat.

I emptied a can of dog food onto a plate and set it on what was to be Bobo's "table," a square of enameled plywood beside the stove. And I put down a dish of water. Bobo walked past them and me as if they and I didn't exist. He went into the studio, dragging the chain. It was a little longer than necessary to reach the bearskin, but not then or ever did he walk to the end of the chain. It was as if, in that way, he denied the humiliating fact that he, who resented a chain anywhere, was being tied up in a house.

Amazingly he was ignoring the lemmings. As usual at this time of day, they were out of their burrows and noisy. Bobo had not even glanced their way. When one gave an especially loud squeak, Bobo's ears would twitch, possibly a reflex action he couldn't control. Though I tried to get his attention, by stooping to talk to him, by bringing his dish of food into the studio, by humming (to assure him, falsely, that I wasn't at all alarmed), Bobo would not meet my eyes. His expressive face clearly showed, however, his feelings of indignation.

The evening grew late. Still Bobo had had no dinner. Once he had gone to the kitchen to drink some water, and came back again to lie on the bear rug. Not once, even yet, had his eyes turned towards the lemmings. I was having real difficulty in concealing my tension. I still hummed, but the purpose now was to quiet my own nervousness. I dreaded to switch off the lights. In a kind of despairing fear, finally, I put them out, and for the rest of a wakeful night listened to the dog interminably licking the gunshot wound in his leg. Apparently Bobo, too, lay awake until morning.

At daybreak he pulled his chain to the door, and I let him out. It seemed doubtful that he would come back. He didn't, all day, and I suspected that I had lost my dog. Yet at dinnertime Bobo was there at the *back* door—he always learned fast. The evening's events repeated those of the night before in every detail: the chain, the rejected food, the elaborate indifference to the lemmings, the refusal to acknowledge that I was there. The following morning, too, he left the house without breakfast. How long would a dog stay on a hunger strike? And why did he come now at all—for the warmth in the house? The well-furred Husky could have endured the outside temperatures of those nights, and if being indoors in my house was so painful, why did he return to it?

A week passed with no change in our routine. I was becoming tired from the loss of sleep and from a growing uneasiness as Bobo's temper seemed to be worsening. He would look at me sometimes now, but with so much fury that every glance seemed like the prelude to an attack.

I decided to ask Dr. Kennedy if he would help me to understand Bobo's mood and perhaps have some suggestions about solving my Husky-lemming conflict of interest. He stopped in on his way home from the office. Dr. Kennedy was a man with a pleasantly unaggressive manner, his slim height seeming to move along almost as if blown by the wind; but his mind was sharp and his skill precise. Bobo lay on the rug when he entered—and for once the dog's eyes returned from their scrutiny of the inward distances. He allowed Dr. Kennedy to examine the wound on his face and the doctor agreed with Ann: evidently the dog had cleaned the wound adequately and his own healing powers were doing the rest. "It's the most impressive regeneration of tissues I've ever seen," he said. "The dog must have amazing vitality."

He knew Bobo, as everyone did, and he was a little disturbed, he said, by the change in his disposition. "I've always thought this was a dog you could trust, but now he's so tense, I don't know. In this mood he'd be unpredictable."

I told him I thought the chain was the difficulty, and he agreed. He also was interested in the lemming experiment, however, and considered it important, and he couldn't think of a better way than the chain to have both the dog and the lemmings in the same house. He predicted that Bobo would accept the chain finally, but meanwhile, he said, "I'm not sure you are safe with him. Don't let him corner you. He's a strong dog. He could do you a lot of harm—the utmost, you know."

He believed that the food problem would solve itself. A dog would not starve through pride. He finished, "Be kind to him but determined. You are having a contest of wills. Don't let Bobo win."

No? And not let him corner me? A house was nothing but a collection of corners! To move around doing the simplest things, I could be trapped in no fewer than seven. I could have shortened the dog's chain, but to limit his freedom still more might perhaps push his anger over the edge.

The problem was clear; I had its dimensions now. To be firm, to be strong of will. I wished I were not so tired.

10

During that night the wind stopped its aimless whirling between the ells of the house and instead became gusty. In the beginning the blasts were not close together, but soon they had picked up speed to sound as if giant hands were slapping, beating the house.

Daylight came slowly and late. The morning was well on towards noon before I could see what I knew was the weather outside: a full-scale, raging blizzard. The scene was a blind white screen that thinned to show vague, shadowed shapes but after a second or two faded out to a white blank again. The snow seemed to be blowing horizontally; yet it was building up on the leeward, street side of the house. There the drifts were seven or eight feet deep before the storm ended.

Bobo went out for no more than a few minutes, blinking into the snow and scratching on the back door to come in again. Then he curled up asleep. During storms he had always been drowsy, and perhaps he was more tired than usual. His recent nights, like my own, had been wakeful, his sleeplessness probably being due to the scent and sound of the nearby lemmings.

After the first three days the road crews gave up the effort to run the snowplows—the only time the streets were impassable in the five years I lived at Nome. The oil trucks no longer could make their rounds, nor the trucks that delivered Nome's water supply from warm springs on the outskirts of town. I was one of those who ran out of water, but with all the snow outside, that problem was quickly solved.

The kitchen cupboard began to show some distressing gaps—no coffee, no salt. There was plenty of meat in the game cache: a hunter had recently given me a forequarter of moose, and the day before the storm started I had bought several pounds of hamburger.

I had met a boy, Bobbie, who had known Sonny's family well, and I told him that Bobo was refusing to eat and asked what my neighbors had fed him.

"Steaks," said Bobbie. "They bought steaks for him."

Since steaks were selling in Nome at $2.25 and $2.75 a pound, I thought it likely that Bobbie was just trying to fix things up for a dog he liked. I did buy some hamburger (at $1.50 a pound) to see whether Bobo's hunger strike could be broken with two or three meals of it.

When I put it down in his dish, Bobo moved his nose over the hamburger, ate a few mouthfuls, and walked away from the rest. A few minutes later, when I unwrapped for myself a moose steak, the scent of the game brought Bobo out to the kitchen with eyes as wild as I'd ever seen them. I ate hamburger for dinner and Bobo ate moose—and he did eat it. When he went back to his bearskin afterwards, he seemed almost relaxed. That night the whole situation seemed hopeful. A quarter of moose would last a long time, and if Bobo was no longer hungry, the tension between us might become easier. I talked to him while I sat doing some mending, and once when he looked up his eyes did not seem to be angry. There was in them almost a suggestion that once our relationship had been happier and might be so again. Had he perhaps begun to accept the humiliation of being chained?

The indoor atmosphere was especially cheerless because one of the workmen had begun to refinish the living-room floor, and the furniture from the other end was piled in the studio section—chairs stacked on the sofa, the phonograph cabinet on top of the china cupboard. During the blizzard the Eskimo didn't come. Eskimos, and white Northerners too, like to sleep through a violent storm, at least in its early stages. After a week or more of such weather a nervousness builds up that makes sleep, day or night, difficult. The continuous roar and the unrelenting slap of the wind become very wearing.

Towards the end of that blizzard two roofs blew off, we heard later, and I began to worry about my windows. Three were large, picture-window size, and double-paned: two downstairs and one in the master bedroom. One of the days, during our brief hours of twilight, I saw that the outer panes were undulating almost as if they were cloth. In Nome many families nail boards across the windows at the start of such storms, and I wished I had done that, for it would be an emergency if one of the downstairs windows should break. We were surrounded by snow too deep, now, for easy escape without snowshoes, which I did not have.

Late that evening there was a shattering crash from above. Both panes of the large upstairs window had blown in; sheets of the glass had sailed through the room and splintered. By the time that I got upstairs, snow was driving across the room to become plastered against the opposite wall, fifteen feet away. I closed the door and went back downstairs, only hop-

ing now that the other windows would hold, and that the
stovepipes would not blow down, nor the power line that
furnished lights and electricity for the fan in the cookstove.
Without electricity the stove would have to be turned off, and
I doubted whether the smaller living-room heater could keep
the indoor temperature above freezing.

It was an anxious time, and Bobo was starting to pick up
my nervousness. The complications were self-inflating. As he
too became high-strung, his anger became more evident, and
then my fears increased and aroused more signs of hostility
in the Husky. One afternoon I happened to glance at the dog
and found that the fur on his shoulders and down the length
of his spine had risen—the same reaction he'd had when
Spider would mince around at the end of the block. To dis-
tract Bobo from whatever sense of outrage had now excited
him, I hurried into the kitchen crying out with enthusiasm,
"Let's have some moose meat!" The meat for his dinner was
only starting to thaw, but I gave it all to him in one piece, and
his chewing up of the frozen chunk (intended originally as a
roast) took him almost an hour. At bedtime I gave him more,
and the next day and thereafter his dish was filled up with
moose meat as soon as he emptied it.

During my various wilderness sojourns there had been a
few slightly threatening situations, and to control my fears
I had found it the best trick to review my notes and natural-
history books in order to think scientifically, and therefore
objectively, about whatever animals then seemed a menace.
(Once it had been a vicious bear and once an irate moose
that took up residence at the door of my cabin.) In the new
and troubled relationship with Bobo it might help if I should
become more analytical about sled dogs and wolves. In the

source material, moreover, I might find something to help with the present problem.

And so I read again how most biologists agree that all dogs are descended from wolves, as proved by the way that their teeth are formed. The teeth of all breeds of dogs are exactly alike except for size, and all are identical in their structure with teeth of wolves. One respected scientist believes that some dogs were evolved from jackals, but his reasoning has not convinced other biologists, since it is hard to explain how jackals' teeth could have been transformed into the quite different wolf-like teeth of those dogs. A further cause for doubt is the fact that jackals have a gland which emits a strong odor extremely repulsive to human noses; and it doesn't seem likely that men, even in ancient times, would have domesticated a foul-smelling animal. Neither Huskies nor Samoyeds, incidentally, have even the different light "doggy smell" to which some people object.

Men must have experimented with animal-breeding fairly soon after their own evolution into a separate species, for the bones of eleven distinct breeds of dogs have been found with the earliest human remains. Egyptian wall decorations done as early as 5000 B.C. show terrier and greyhound types. Four thousand years ago Pekingese were almost the same as that breed today, and spaniels were being imported from Spain to England before the Christian era. These are the records; we can only surmise how many centuries it took to breed a terrier or a Pekingese out of animals like wild wolves—and can only surmise why any particular type of dog was wanted. It is easy to guess that dogs would have been bred to increase their strength to pull loads, or their keen noses to aid in hunting, and that the silken Chinese aristocrats would have liked silken-furred dogs, which they produced eventually in the Pekingese. But surely a sense of humor, too, was functioning the way that human beings "designed" some of their dogs—humor and an interest in the exotic.

The word *dog* itself comes from the Anglo-Saxon *docga*, for which the earlier root is not known. Anyone who experiments, however, will find that the sound of the *o* in *dog* carries farther than almost any other sound that can be uttered by human vocal cords, and we can speculate that *dog*, or *docga*, originated as an effective call for the animals. "Here, boss," used in the United States to summon cows, has the same *o* sound in *boss*, and close to it is the *o* in the word *cow* itself.

Many names of individual breeds of dogs are derived from the place where they were developed: spaniels, salukis, great Danes, Kerry blues, and Chihuahuas.

The name *Husky* does not refer to the dogs' size or strength, but is a corruption of *Esky*, the slang designation for Eskimos used by some of the early white travelers to their country. The Northern dogs, then called Esky dogs, finally became "Huskies." When a breed's name is derived from the name of a tribe or people, it usually is capitalized, as Husky, Samoyed, and Malemute. The Malemutes or, as formerly spelled, Malemiuts, were a tribe of Eskimos living around Kotzebue Sound.

The earliest Huskies are thought to have been developed from wolves in the Stone Age. Skeletons of those dogs were unearthed during the building of the Ladoga Canal near the border of Finland and Russia. They would, of course, have been a modification of Northern wolves. Dogs of a similar strain were being used in Alaska more than twelve thousand years ago—whether brought there by Eskimos from Siberia or whether developed from local wolves is not known. The Siberian Huskies like Bobo are a quite recent import. The first time that any number were seen in Alaska was during the 1890's. That was the period when the United States Government was buying Siberian reindeer for the Alaska Eskimos, as a possible food supply to replace the whales that had been depleted to furnish whalebone for women's corsets. Travel and trade were brisk between the two continents then, and the Siberian Eskimos found that their Huskies had a high barter value. They were recognized as a strain of sled dogs superior in strength and temperament to the Alaska Malemutes.

In color most Malemutes are grizzled or brownish, with the characteristic dark patches around their eyes described usually as masks. True Siberians lack the masks and are clear white, black, and gray, their fur in most cases being shorter and smoother than Malemutes'. In some of their body structures the Siberians suggest the light-colored Samoyeds, another Siberian breed, causing some speculation that the Siberian Huskies might have originated as a mixture of Samoyeds and black Northern wolves. The black wolves are always more sleek than the others. The arctic is also the home of white and of gray wolves, however, and possibly the Siberian Huskies represent only a combination of wild-wolf strains.

The distinction between wolves and Huskies must be a remarkably fuzzy line in the minds of Eskimos—as it is fuzzy in fact. No other dogs except Huskies are still being bred consistently with the wild wolves that were the ancestors of all dogs. It is not strange then that only Huskies have the true wolf characteristics, in build, shape of face, approximate size, color, and such physiological details as sharp pointed ears, slanting eyes, and full-furred tails. That they also have some of the best qualities of the wolf temperament is well known to all who understand Huskies. The white settlers who own Huskies tend to be people who are at home with wild nature. They are biologists, wilderness guides, trappers, ardent hunters and fishermen, and they value the very traits in their dogs that require some adjusting on the part of the human companion. How it works out I was still to learn in the association with Bobo.

No white man I've ever met is as much at home in the natural scene as an Eskimo is—any Eskimo, men and women down to the child who is learning his first words, which are probably names of animals. (In the Eskimo dialect of the Yukon delta the word for dog is *Ki-mukh-ta*.) All wild animals fascinate Eskimos, but especially wolves do.

One of my friends from an Eastern city was visiting in Alaska and spent an evening in one of the Eskimo cabins. It seemed poor and bleak to her, and she was feeling pity for the young native wife. They had been talking about a trip the Eskimo girl once made to Fairbanks, but she changed the subject abruptly—for the reason perhaps that she sensed the visitor's pity and wanted to turn the tables. Speaking about the experience that to her would be supreme, she asked,

"Did you ever hunt wolves by moonlight?"

At the question the visitor's mind may have flashed a composite picture of her so-civilized life, including her drawing room with its glassed indoor garden and two grand pianos. No, she said, she never had hunted wolves. Now the pity was on the Eskimo's face. She shook her head sympathetically:

"You have not hunted wolves in the moonlight—you have not lived!"

The white woman, who had seen the girl driving a dog sled, asked if any of the dogs in the team were part wolf.

"I would not have a dog that was not part wolf," the girl replied. Why? "Wolf dogs are more cute."

"Do you mean darling, pretty?"

"Not darling—sharp."

The Eskimo had used *cute* in its original sense of *acute*: keen, perceiving. And when the girl spoke of hunting wolves, she not only meant adult wolves, whose long shoulder fur is used for the ruffs on most parki hoods; she probably also was thinking of the wolf pups she always would hope to find in order to introduce their strain into the dogs of her team.

There is small difficulty in getting wolves and Huskies to mate (the breeding is most often successful if the wolf is the bitch), but Huskies generally are reluctant to mate with outside dogs. Dr. Charles R. Stockard, till his death the authority on canine genetics, had so many failures in trying to cross Huskies with other breeds that he said, "Huskies don't seem to recognize the more highly domesticated dogs as being their own species."

An Eskimo who wants to strengthen the wolf strain in his team may capture a grown wolf, but it usually is thought easier to raise the wolf in captivity, and wolf pups are not hard to find in dens in the spring.

Actually all Huskies have a large intermixture of wolf blood. If they had been bred with outside dogs frequently, the Huskies' wolf characteristics would have become diluted, but most Huskies are mated with other Huskies; and a dog that is quarter wolf, when bred with another quarter wolf, for example, will have pups that are still quarter wolf. As long as the Husky line remains pure, the wolf component is still there.

It is a question whether the wolf blood in Northern dogs is being bred out of them at the present time. My own guess is that it isn't. Most Huskies originate in the native teams, and those dogs would be mated with wild wolves more often than they would be with outside dogs. In the Eskimo village, Unalakleet, there were more than five hundred dogs when I was there. All were Huskies except a cocker spaniel owned by the teacher, and he was a house pet and didn't thin out the wolf strain of any team. During the same year there was at least one Husky litter out of a wolf.

In associating with people and in coping with human problems, Huskies acquire some mental abilities that would not be found in the wild. But the Huskies lose something, too, a degree of sharpness. Friends of mine own both a wolf and a Husky, and they have discovered that when the wolf gets her chain wound around a post, she will unwind herself, but the Husky, although a very smart dog, does not do that, nor does any other Husky I've ever known.

The wolf trait that is most valuable, in a leader especially, is the homing instinct. It is much stronger in Huskies with recent wolf ancestors. Young Wilfred Ryan, son of the Eskimo postmaster at Unalakleet, was out on his trapline one day when a blinding blizzard blew up. Wilfred was not dressed warmly enough to sit it out in a snow shelter. He would have to travel a distance of thirty miles, with the snow so dense that he could not see any dogs of his team from the sled. Such a blizzard effaces all signs of a trail within minutes, and the driver, unable to check his landmarks, must give the lead dog entire responsibility for bringing home man and team.

Throughout the village there was concern about Wilfred, because his team would be following a route on the frozen Unalakleet River, and at the river's mouth the lead dog would have to make a right-angle turn to the settlement on the beach. If the dog didn't, the team would continue out over the sea ice, only two miles farther to open water where, without warning, all would go over the edge. Darkness fell and the blizzard thickened. Frank, Wilfred's father, was less worried than most because, he said, "My leader is half wolf, and so he will not miss the turn." And he didn't. About nine o'clock the eleven tired but excited dogs arrived back at the door of Frank's cabin. Wilfred was cold but safe.

Husky leaders have been known to find the way home with their eyes swollen completely shut from snow-blindness, an inflammation caused by the dazzling light of the newly returned sun on the glazed white landscape. Such a dog would be useless unless he had the wolf's intuition that guides his steps in the right direction.

There are other emergencies when a wolf's acuteness is needed in Eskimos' lead dogs. Sometimes the ice on the arctic rivers is weakened by overflows. A snowfall will hide the danger. The man would not guess it was there, but a good leader will know and will guide the sled safely around it. Dogs also are used on the sea ice, to smell out the breathing holes of seals, to pull the hunter to open water where seals may be swimming, to track polar bears, and for other trips that take them away from land. The sea ice is never safe. Cracks may open under a man or a sled any time; and yesterday's crack may have a light coating of insecure ice concealed by fresh snow. A good leader will sense the danger and, again, turn in another direction. Trails sometimes follow along the snow cornices at the sides of rivers. There comes a day, every spring, when the cornice which still looks safe would no longer support a sled. From that day the leader will not venture onto it, even though he may be ignoring the driver's commands.

Command is not quite the right word when an Eskimo drives the team. The driver, often using the name of the leader, calls, "Mush, Star!" or *gee, haw,* or *whoa.* (Those particular words were borrowed from white men accustomed to driving horses. Formerly every Eskimo driver had his own set of calls, which gave him a greater sense that the team was peculiarly his.) These words are not orders so much as suggestions, in that the lead dog knows he may either agree or refuse to follow them. The hunter that rides the runners submerges his own will to that of his leader—all the way. It is an attitude that some white owners of teams for sport find it hard to learn, and if their safety is not involved, they can of course take a more authoritative attitude with their dogs. An Eskimo has so little impulse to dominate other people, he has so modest and co-operative an approach in all relationships, that he can more gracefully put himself in the care of his Husky leader.

The Eskimo and his leader are not master and servant or slave. They are comrades who trust and need and respect each other. They are not very demonstrative—an affectionate touch, a word (and the "word" may be the dog's, too): these are sometimes the only signs, but no one can see a hunter and lead dog together without knowing that there is a deeply-felt bond between them, and that their minds are communicating in a free, sensitive way.

If an arctic hunter becomes incapacitated—ill or injured

or unconscious from cold—the lead dog if possible still must get him home. It is essential then that he have the innate qualities to command. At all other times, too, in making his quick decisions, the lead dog must have authority over the Huskies behind him, but especially if his driver would not be able to help straighten out a rebellious team. The team must obey without question—or if they don't, the leader himself must be able to handle the situation. Once when Olivia Westcott's team got away from her, Chena, her half-wolf leader, had to control a group of unruly dogs that wanted to bolt. Chena solved his dilemma by turning around and climbing onto the sled himself. The lines then were tangled so hopelessly that the team could not move in any direction.

Since there can be no divided loyalty in a hunter's team, an Eskimo driver has almost no personal relationship with any of his dogs except the leader. He probably throws each one a fish every day and he handles them when he puts them in harness. There his influence and his association with the dogs end. They are the leader's dogs, not the driver's, and they must not be given a chance to make any mistake about the arrangement. The driver may even seem cruel to the lesser dogs; he may actually be cruel at times. Perhaps the harsh treatment is necessary. The man's own instinct may be working there, telling him to break up any affection, devotion to him personally, that a team dog might be developing.

These dogs behind the leader are also part wolf. In them, as in wolves, is the freedom of the untrammeled winds; action, speed, distance—these are their need and delight. And yet most of the time, many months in the year, they have no activity except what they can get on the end of a five-foot chain. They often are hungry. Their intense longing to hunt is not given expression in all their lives. They have a wolf's instinct for family relationships, which is never fulfilled, and a dog's longing to be petted and loved, and that too they are denied. With these frustrations and hardships it is not strange that late in the winter, when the weather induces an extra tension, some dogs may suddenly have an urge to attack human beings. Men go berserk every day under conditions that seem less trying.

As for real wolves killing humans, on this continent it has happened so seldom that for many years no biologist would accept any of the tales as authentic. The few now in question have brought up the likelihood that the wolves involved had contracted rabies, a disease they are known to have at times (as do foxes and other wild animals). There have been so many contacts between wolves and men that surely many more attacks would have occurred if wolves actually had a taste for human flesh. The Eskimos say that wolf-dogs are more dangerous than wild wolves. If true, the reason doubtless would be that the wolf temperament in those dogs is put under strains which become intolerable.

Mankind once recognized wolves as friends; otherwise they would not have been taken in to share human hearths. We are the poorer that somewhere along in history men lost sight of the wolves' integrity and co-operation and tenderness.

The relationship of the followers to the lead dog probably gives them some satisfaction. Among the wolves that association would be expressed in many ways; the team dogs as followers have the single fulfillment of galloping where their leader wants them to gallop, but undoubtedly there is a sense of devotion—going both ways—if a team is well organized. Reports of the dog teams the military took to the antarctic were harrowing to those who know Huskies well. Inexperienced handlers had assembled teams with little if any regard for the natural grouping of loyal Husky followers behind a strong and magnetic leader; and from the published accounts it seems evident that the men rather enjoyed the discord among the team members. A good Husky team is not a haphazard collection of muscular and aggressive dogs.

An authentic leader knows when his team is becoming too tired, and he will slow his pace or will work out some ruse to make his driver halt the run for a little while. The lead dog invariably pulls his own share of the load, and usually more than his share: whether traveling or at rest he will keep the lead-line, to which all the other dogs' lines are attached, straight and taut. The sense of responsibility born in a lead dog functions not only towards the driver and his needs but also towards the dogs following him and *their* needs.

With so much required of a leader it is no wonder that talented dogs like these occur rarely. Perhaps one puppy in thirty to fifty will show the traits watched for so eagerly. He will show them early. By the time that the dogs in a litter are six weeks old, it may be seen that one always takes the initiative in their romping. He will be the most bold. He both encourages the attentions of the others and checks them if they offend him. If the several dogs are sharing one food dish, the puppy leader is given first place, usually without having to demand it, but he will demand it if necessary. When the puppies start to run around free, they do not explore as a group of quite independent dogs, but as one strong-willed dog and his followers. The Eskimo owner, watching with something like awe at his good luck, will say, "Maybe too soon to be sure, but I think I have leader, this bunch of puppies." And he will pick up the small Husky and fondle it, the first of many actions that will encourage the leader's sense that he is unique and important, as the man searches the blunt little face that even then, somehow, does not look young.

These were the facts and comments, written into my notebooks at Unalakleet, that came back to light in the days when the storm shut up Bobo and me unhappily in the gloomy room, when the chain clanked across the floor every time Bobo moved, till it bothered me almost as much as it did the dog, days while the lemmings fought one another and ran their wheel with an endless metallic clicking of claws on wire mesh.

When I finished rereading the notes, I looked down at Bobo, whose rug was beside my chair, and marveled that any animal could have had such restraint. Surrounded with provocations that must have been almost unbearable to a Husky dog, he had not once given in to his exasperation. On the day that the fur on his back was bristling, he may have been close to his breaking point. We weathered that climax, after which he had seemed more resigned than indignant.

The storm was diminishing as these thoughts finally were sorted out. The time was evening, about eight o'clock. I reached down and unsnapped Bobo's chain. He didn't look up. He showed no surprise. But he slowly rose and with dignity walked to the door—the front door, on the way passing within two feet of the lemming cage and not even turning his head. I let him out and he did not come back that night. He was gone for several days. Then one afternoon when I came home from a walk to the post office, Bobo was there, at the front door again. Inside, he ignored the lemmings, lay down on the bearskin, with a deep sigh relaxed, and soon was asleep.

11

Was it possible that lemmings were not, after all, attractive to Bobo? Had the indoor chain been unnecessary during those troubled weeks? Now that Bobo was free in the house, he still paid no attention to the small juicy rodents. The first time he had come, on the rope, his excitement at seeing them had been as frantic as any animal could express. When he smelled the wild moose meat, later, he had shown a little of the same overwhelming urge, though it wasn't as strong as when he discovered the lemmings—naturally, since the lemmings were alive and would trigger his impulse to hunt and pounce. Could an urge so clearly inborn simply cease to function?

One could guess that a careful training program might teach a very co-operative dog that he could not have something he so intensely, instinctively wanted. Even then, would he not control only his actions and not his interest? When the lemmings were darting around in plain sight and chirring, no animal, not even one that never caught mice, could have failed to see them. Yet this Husky, this domesticated wolf, appeared in every way not to know they were there.

For the next few weeks after the storm Bobo and I lived in the house happily and harmoniously. We worked out our

joint schedules, his coming and going and mine, our meal-
times, the number of hours we both slept at night, which in
that season were nearly the same. All these arrangements are
part of owning a dog as of having children: if it is too early at
night when they go to sleep, they will wake up too early. With
a dog also the program must be adjusted.

I thought that it was till I happened to realize that Bobo
was not going to sleep when the evening was over. As I
learned one night when I too stayed awake, after about an
hour Bobo got up from his bearskin quietly and went out into
the entrance hall and up the stairs. I never had known him
to go up before, nor did he then until he might suppose I had
had time to become unconscious of what he was doing. His
leaving the room was so silent as to seem stealthy, but he
could not prevent the click of his claws on the uncarpeted
stairway.

He stayed up there for fifteen or twenty minutes. Then he
came down, still very quietly, and returned to his rug.

The next night and for several weeks curiosity kept me
awake to see whether Bobo's trip up the stairs was a regular
happening. It was, though I had to lie motionless for some
time, feigning sleep, before Bobo would make his start. The
stir . . . the measured clicking, step above step . . . the long
wait with no sound . . . the clicking again, a little heavier
as he let his weight down the steps . . . his movement back
into the room, more felt than heard, the sinking of breath and
body onto the fur of his rug, his tongue stroking along his
foreleg a few times . . . he sighs, and then stillness.

What did it mean?

After many of those nights, in which his routine was never
broken, barefoot, silently, as I thought, I followed Bobo as

far as the landing. From one of the round tower windows a crooked circle of moonlight fell on the floor of the upstairs hall. It was reflected on Bobo's white face and ruff as he hovered over the edge of the door to the lemmings' room. He was sniffing, up and down one side, then the other side, back and forth at the base of the doorway, sniffing, sniffing endlessly and with desperate-seeming motions as if he were ravenous for the lemmings' scent.

I left, realizing too late that I should not have spied upon him, and for his pride's sake hoping that he had not heard me.

Had he?

The following night he did not go up the stairs, nor the night after that, nor ever again as far as I knew.

It is a sad thing to look back and know that one has so crassly blundered. For by wilderness values it was inexcusable to have ripped the covering off the dog's secret. How could I compensate? Only in some way that would respect wild integrity. The next day I went out for several hours and left Bobo alone in the house with the lemming cage. Trusting him was my apology. I knew that when I came home I would find the lemmings unharmed, and they were. Bobo had led me a few short steps into his world. I would go further, but would have to learn first how to tread more delicately.

Though I did understand the way Eskimos treat the dogs of their teams, it became evident when I acquired Bobo that no one has worked out the rules of behavior for a single Husky that lives in a civilized household. The families that owned the other members of Bobo's pack must have solved the problem, but they were people that so far I didn't know, and of course their Huskies weren't leaders. Since a team leader isn't subservient to any man, and the other dogs only obey a Husky, compliance with human commands is not in the inheritance of these dogs. Yet a Husky kept as a pet has to learn to obey in a few situations—doesn't he?

Huskies are born housebroken. Wild wolves keep their burrows clean, and Huskies are close enough to those instincts to respect the burrows their owners inhabit. That kind of training then isn't required. They are not born with a willingness to walk on leashes, to heel, to sit, to come, to lie down, to wait, nor of course to do any tricks. I personally dislike seeing dogs do tricks, but I thought that my Bobo should agree to a few other things that I'd want of him. Some day I would be taking him on a trip to large cities. Could I walk with him on Fifth Avenue in New York if he'd never accepted a leash? Could I visit friends with him if he had not been taught to sit or lie quietly, if he were not a well-behaved dog? On that training I thought we should start early in our association, and the time seemed right when the indoor chain and my spying upon the dog were, as I hoped, forgotten.

We would begin with the leash, attached to a new choke collar which in theory would make any rebellious straining uncomfortable for the dog. It was a brisk winter afternoon when we set out for the lesson. But as soon as we reached the bottom step, Bobo sat down. He didn't seem angry, only preoccupied, having become suddenly fascinated by the roofline of Mr. Kasson's house. Gently I tugged at the leash, but the roofline had become of hypnotic interest—until very abruptly Bobo decided that no, he wanted to bolt. He shot away at a speed that landed me on my head, fortunately on a walk that was padded with snow. When I got on my feet again, Bobo resumed his study of architecture.

We tried to outwait each other. For as long as I would

stand still Bobo would sit still; at my first step he took ten, hurling forward all his sixty-five pounds of strength. We stopped, we made those explosive starts. After half an hour we had progressed almost half a block.

I never could punish Bobo, not with all the scars he had hidden under his fur. But there had to be some way to induce his obedience, and to give or withhold food might be the answer, I thought. So far there was nothing for which to reward him, but plenty for which to reprimand. I gave him no dinner that night, being quite sure he would understand why. No doubt he did, but not then or ever would food or the lack of it prove a lever. Huskies, at least some of them, are not enough interested in food for an owner to use it effectively in their training. The same thing has been true of Tunerak. "Teach him to come when you blow a whistle by blowing it every time you feed him and by having a bite of meat as a reward when he answers it in the field": that was the helpful advice of my veterinary, but with Tunerak, as with Bobo, the problem is not how to create an association in the dog's mind between food and obedience, but to get the food down at any time. Both dogs have lost their appetites over the slightest emotional upset such as a clash of wills. Tunerak even loses a previous meal if I scold him.

After many tries I did persuade Bobo to walk on the end of a twenty-five-foot rope. He would move if he had twenty-five feet of freedom, but he'd move up on people's porches, in and out of the timbers supporting oil tanks, behind garbage cans, and around and around telephone poles—entangling himself in any obstruction that would make me appear foolish in getting him out. If I pulled in the rope by as much as five feet, Bobo commenced his sitting and bolting routine. He was not giving in at all; he was only choosing to win in a different way, and so ingeniously that I was convinced the dog had a sense of humor.

We gave up the leash training on New Year's Eve. Due to aerial icing conditions Nome had not had a plane come in for three weeks. All our holiday mail arrived on that day. Joyfully, with a handful of letters, I came out of the post office, untied Bobo's rope from the flagpole and started home. But my dog made a headlong dash that threw me off balance, and the unopened Christmas mail whirled away on the wind, forever lost on the snowy width of the frozen sea.

Perhaps we should postpone the teaching of mere manners until we were better acquainted. There were a few practical situations, however, in which it seemed absolutely necessary for him to take orders.

He would have liked to finish his last greasy bone while he relaxed on the bearskin. After his meal in the kitchen, with a self-possessed stride he would carry the bone to the living room. Always I took it away from him and the next night he'd bring in another one. Having the bone to chew probably was not as important to him as his independence, his self-respect as a Husky who made the decisions.

We could dispute the bones, but we couldn't dispute his lying upon the caribou skins, which were spread over the living-room floor now that it was refinished. Caribou skins, the winter hides, are gray and chalk-white, deep and soft and as dense as the thickest plush. They are beautiful to see and no doubt pleasant to rest upon—but they shed. The white hairs are of different structure, fragile tubes which contain air and are probably good insulation for the caribou. They break off at a touch however, and sometimes, I suspected, of their own electrical charge.

Every time Bobo dropped down on one of the skins, his weight snapped off countless hairs, which immediately attached themselves to his coat. I have seen them rise from the rug and jump into his fur, which may have been even more highly electrified, and I have seen them jump from Bobo's coat to the wool of my skirt, although Bobo had not touched the skirt in passing. But the scattering of the hairs was mainly accomplished by Bobo's shaking himself every time he got up from a rug. There were hairs in my typewriter, hairs in the soup, hairs in my hair: by some means the caribou rugs must be made taboo.

It was doubtless my desperation about the hairs that made Bobo see them as a possibility to turn into an issue. In the beginning when I told him to get up off the rugs, often he would. Then, when he realized that here was a fine chance to assert his authority, with perverse shrewdness, it seemed, he used them as a means of rebellion. He himself never began our controversies; he waited until I had denied him something he wanted. In his dinner some night was there not enough lean meat, which he knew I knew he preferred? Straight to a caribou rug. Did I drive away from the house without taking him? I knew where I'd find him when I came back. Did he decide that on this day he would like to go into the butcher shop, where dogs weren't allowed, and I left him outside? He pushed past me to get to a caribou rug when we returned to our house. And the bone routine had a new wrinkle. He carried the bone from the kitchen to his bearskin, as usual; I removed it, as usual; whereupon Bobo moved to one of the other, forbidden rugs.

The clash of wills was becoming a clamor. Bobo spent part of each day on a shelf in the bay window of the entrance hall. He had the trait, typical of wolves, of being curious about everything, not only those affairs that normally interest a dog. From the window he could watch snowplows, children playing (when he was not with them), the cars and the people passing, and the dogs. Although far from being enough recovered to challenge the Huskies, and far, therefore, from being able to lead them, in the window he could growl at them safely and ferociously. He could get his dander to working again.

There also were flower pots on that window sill. Bobo could thread his way through them as adroitly as any cat. One day he knocked one of them over. I scolded him. The next day several were upset. I put a chair on the stairway landing, from which he went onto the shelf. Bobo jumped over the chair, into the middle of the pots, most of which crashed to the floor.

If I insisted on treating him like a dog, he would have something to say about that. Nobody thwarts a leader.

In the arctic one's dreaming is apt to plunge or soar into supernatural realms. The width of the treeless horizon, the earthbound clouds, resting upon the hills but with breaks that open out into celestial light, the towering ridges of ice on the ocean: these we see in the daytime and so these we dream of at night . . . and the dreams are peopled with beings never met on Front Street or Second Avenue.

It was on one of those far wanderings, on a deep black night in February, that the dream was penetrated by a voice so feral and so overpowering in its volume that I woke in cold terror.

The voice continued, a call meant by nature to fill all of a landscape and now reverberating between four close walls. It took a few moments to realize that the voice was not that of a spirit calling from some larger earth, but was Bobo's.

Up to that time Bobo had not been one of the more vocal Huskies. I had heard his voice a few times as he bayed in unison with his followers, but not alone. Immersed, drowned as I was in the darkness there by the sound, I thought, If mountains could sing, their voices would be like this, full, rich, and resonant against the dome of the sky.

Had Bobo himself been dreaming, perhaps that he was a wolf, singing up on a hilltop, and had his real voice carried on the song? For a song it certainly was, musical, with tones that seemed as pure as a human's, and yet just as certainly it was communication. He may have been trying to call to the family who had left him a few months earlier—gone where, Bobo knew not. Or was he in fact trying to say what I hadn't been understanding in our numerous disagreements over chains and lemmings, bone, rugs, and window flowers? There was indeed a meaning, a reason for the discord in our house, but I hadn't been grasping it.

When Bobo's song ended I spoke to him; he answered; I replied. It was the first of many such conversations between us, and what came out of this one for me was the morning memory of a haunting experience, and a sense that the Husky was troubled and was trying to convey to someone, somewhere, a burden that lay on his heart.

After breakfast he wanted to leave the house, but the air was filled with a lashing sleet; it would have turned his coat into an armor of ice, and his recovery was not yet complete enough for such weather trials. After he'd had a moment outdoors I pulled him back inside, and since it was his wish to do something else, he rebuked me by going to lie on a caribou rug.

I drew a footstool close to the rug and sat down and talked to him:

"Bobo, if we're going to live here happily in this house, you should be willing to give up your way sometimes, even if you are a leader.

"It wouldn't give me any satisfaction to order you to do this and that. But the caribou hairs are intolerable, and we do want the flowers, and even you wouldn't like your bearskin after you'd eaten a lot of bones on it. If you understood these things, I don't think you'd object to what I ask. Would you?"

At the rising inflection, the query, Bobo answered. He lifted his head and the same long, troubled cadence that he had sung in the night wound out of his throat—a quick slide up to a high tone, held to a pervasive length; then gliding down slowly, the voice came up into a little rise again, with a final slipping down into a sigh.

Whether the next words were a response to his voice, or came out of that caldron that does, sometimes, boil our thoughts away to their essence, I heard myself say, "Maybe the answer is that I should *ask* you to do things, not tell you. Would you go and lie on the bearskin now, instead of this brittle caribou fur, if I said please, Bobo?"

It no longer seems incredible, so accustomed did I become to Bobo's reaction to "please," that he did get up from the caribou fur and went to the bearskin, where he dropped his head onto his forepaws and looked up with oblique, slightly mocking eyes.

Again, it is not necessary to believe that Bobo comprehended the exact words. By that time, of course, he knew well that it was defiance to lie on the caribou rugs. My manner now was conciliatory; well then, he would match the courtesy.

All our conflicts were solved with that simple word, "please." It was not the word that was important, but the way it was said—so that it granted Bobo the right to comply or refuse. It took a little practice to get it just right, for the "please" had to be spoken with an "if" in it: "Will you—if you please?" The question had to be there and sincerely. An irritable command with a "please" tacked onto the end of it didn't work.

"Will you give in to me on this business of not taking bones out of the kitchen—please?" Ever after, Bobo would carry his treasured bone to the very threshold of the kitchen door but there drop it, with a long-suffering glance over his shoulder.

"Since I love to have flowers here in this wintry window, won't you please be careful not to knock them over?" He was.

"It would only cause trouble if I took you into the butcher shop, and so you will wait outside, won't you—please?" He did.

Bobo enjoyed any walk that we took together so much that he had been in the habit of jumping against me impulsively when I put on my boots and parki. "I'll have to stop Bobo's doing this," I said one evening when we were going out with the editor of the Eskimo newspaper.

"When he jumps up on you, step on his hind feet," said Gene. But that would have seemed a crude way to teach any-

thing to this Husky! I made sure that I had the dog's attention and then said, "Please don't jump like this any more, ever
—will you not, Bobo?"

He never did, although the restraint was misery for him.
In delighted anticipation he would bound around, turning in
my direction from one side and then the other, but checking
his leap every time.

"Please" simply recognized Bobo's share in this household.
With that really nice dog, one that preferred to co-operate,
I had nothing to lose by agreeing with Bobo that he should
make some of the choices.

I had nothing to lose and much to gain by giving Bobo
some leeway to react in civilized situations. Here was a voice,
almost unspoiled in its wildness, speaking to human beings,
nature's so-alienated children, about the lives we have set up
for ourselves with our new talent, intelligence. I have always
believed that nature has many valuable things to say to us,
even remote as we are from her now. If she does, nature
could have no better spokesman than Bobo.

12

After his victory Bobo moved through the house with a self-possession that was majestic. Was this indeed my house, or only a rather large dog house that he graciously let me share? I had had to give in on the food question, too. Bobo would now eat beef, as well as moose, if it was lean and not mixed with anything else. I put into his dish a Husky's portion of broth and beef from a stew, omitting the vegetables since he had made it clear that he didn't like them. He lapped up the broth and ate all the meat, and when he walked away, there together on one side of his dish were two small disdained peas—in case I thought I was putting anything over on him.

I had a dog now; he could be left alone with the lemmings quite safely, and if he was not indoors at night, he was near and probably he was watching the house. It might be expecting too much of a Husky, but I wished there were also more warmth, more companionship in our association. Bobo would lie near my chair in a way so reticent, so unresponsive that it seemed both to acknowledge and to deny that a bond was growing between us. Perhaps that was his feeling: yes and no. He had been offended so deeply—a *leader* not trusted!—that he could not quickly put himself on a basis of friendliness.

Nevertheless, in some way mysterious and intangible, he

had become a valuable flywheel to my temperament. It was not only that he was rebellious unless treated with courtesy—the manners around that house had become gentle enough to have been acceptable at the Court of St. James's; but also Bobo seemed to absorb and smooth out the ups and downs of the authorship process.

At the times when a writer must grope in the gray, clouded, and stifling region where images and ideas can be so elusive, a tension builds up. At those times Bobo too became tense. Now he could not lie still, his nighttime sleep was broken, even as mine was, and his appetite declined at the same time that mine did. He had picked up so much of my nervousness that it seemed heartless to make him share it. With his instinct for balance, however, he fought it better than I did, and when he had relaxed again, my own creative energies seemed to come under that influence. It would be hard to estimate how much he contributed to the writing of two of my longer books, but the amount certainly was not little.

This help didn't seem proof of any affection in Bobo, not in view of the dog's aloof manner. He never expressed openly any pleasure that I was there, nor made any appeal for loving attention from me. Sometimes his forehead was knotted up, with an ache in the scars perhaps, and then I always wished I might try to stroke it away. But he did not appear to welcome that kind of sympathy. I wondered if it was fair to keep him, if I shouldn't give him to someone else. With his face healing so well, there must be many who would be glad to have him, and among them there must be one, surely, of whom he could be more fond.

Late one afternoon, then, the Nome physician came to the house to diagnose a severe pain in my shoulder. It was the onset of shingles, he said, and a room was available at the hospital if I'd like to go back with him. I thought I could cope with the illness at home. "We'll reserve a room on the chance that you change your mind," he said.

The moon was full that night and I put Bobo out, for a full moon made him restless and he liked to roam around, baying. By the time that I let him go, about ten o'clock, the pain had become gruesome, but it hadn't occurred to me that I should keep the dog with me. Almost immediately, however, he scratched on the door.

I let him in and sat down in the chair where I had been rocking to ease the anguish. Bobo surprisingly put his head in my lap, something he never had done before, and he looked up with a face that mirrored my torment. Next he lay down with his chin across one of my feet, and later, when I could sit still no longer, he paced up and down the room at my side and, as we walked, often touched my hand with his nose. For the entire sleepless night he poured out his sympathy, in one way and another, so continually that there was never a moment when I could feel alone.

Though it appeared that Bobo's affection was born, fully developed, during those hours, something like it must have existed already. Could that have been the reason why he returned every day to the chain that was such a humiliation? And why he came later to a house where someone tried to defeat his will? Some attachment must have been there; yet his pride as a Husky and as a leader would not let him be sentimental, would not let him look up at anyone with his heart in his eyes, or fawn around human feet.

Both of us, being somewhat reserved and unrevealing of ourselves, had found it hard to bring about the good feeling that our early acquaintance had promised. It was Bobo, breaking out of his normal aloofness, who crossed the gap. Not moved by his need, but mine, he had come all the way—with the kind of affection that many dogs would be able to give, but in Bobo's case it was expressed with a Husky leader's initiative.

Bobo and I were insatiable walkers. In winter we walked in town, and sometimes beyond on a ploughed road to the mining-company's dredges, with the smooth white tundra around us, sweeping up to the white hills against the sky. In summer we walked on those hills and on the wide, shining beach when the tide was out. As we left the door Bobo would bound ahead to the boardwalk and then always turn back to touch my hand with his nose: such a spilling-over of joy that he had to express it with more than a sweeping of tail and a prance of feet.

At other times, too, during the course of the walk, he would brush my hand, always coming up from behind with a flash of speed and turning his head so that his nose crossed my glove. If he had been taught to walk on a leash there would have been no such spontaneous little hellos, and many times I was glad he had ruled against any leash-training. I am grateful to have the memory of him stepping along with the white tip of his plume bouncing over his back, a dog jaunty and independent, utterly free except when love made him conform to a human's needs.

I am sure that his nose-touch at first was expressing his own wish and impulse. Gradually it appeared that he also dashed by for a different reason, a response to a thought of mine: where is Bobo? He ranged out away from the road rather widely. Sometimes he was lost from sight behind snow-drifts or, in summer, deep in the marsh grass. I had only to wonder whether he'd gone very far: an instant later the re-assuring touch came like an answer.

Bobo had also worked out a way of putting across his own thought. During the first months that he lived in my house he would stand by the door and perhaps raise his voice when he wished to go out. If he was thirsty or hungry, he noisily rattled his dish for water or the one for food. After a while he did nothing so obvious. He would come and, facing me squarely, would fasten his eyes on mine with a gaze I inter-preted as, "Please give me your help and, if you don't mind, right now." That much was easy to understand; more remark-able was the fact that his eyes could convey what he wanted. The day came rather soon when I never opened the door if what Bobo demanded was water; and never gave him a drink if it was food he was asking for. I "just knew," or rather, Bobo's eyes could "just tell me." When he wished to come in from outdoors, not even the gaze was necessary. Usually pre-occupied, thinking of something else, I would go to the door, on which he no longer scratched, and invariably would find him there.

He could waken me with his eyes, and did, all too often. He could stand two or three feet away from the bed and, by concentrating his gaze on my eyelids, he could force them to open. The experience of being pulled out of a deep dream by the intensity of an animal's eyes was nearly as startling at first as being awakened by Bobo's song. Later I came to think that if one had to be roused, eyes would be one of the gentlest alarms.

As the spring advanced, however, the sun rose at five, four, three, and finally one o'clock, and Bobo's eagerness to be up and out arose with it. By then I was spending the nights upstairs. When I went up Bobo usually was asleep in the studio, but he would rouse after I had gone and would follow. One morning, unable to sleep again after the trip down to let him out, I decided that when I left the studio in the evening I would close the door into the entrance hall and prevent his coming upstairs. That night, for the first time, Bobo went to sleep in that doorway. In getting past him of course I wakened him. On every subsequent night Bobo foiled my plan—interesting enough in itself, but also he seemed to know why I'd wanted to leave him downstairs. For he never again woke me up with his gaze. He spent the nights in my room, on a black bearskin rug, but he didn't stir in the morning till I did. He stayed on the rug, although his eyes always were open when I first opened mine.

Finally it came to seem that Bobo had access to almost anything that was in my mind. During the hours of every day spent in writing, I would stop occasionally to relax for a few moments. At times when the subject came to a natural break, I would go out of doors and sit on the steps. The breaks were quite unpredictable—there might be forty minutes between them or three hours, since the recess was always determined by the material in the typewriter. From the boardwalk, or the top of a snowdrift in winter, where Bobo spent most of his day, he could not see me inside, for his head would be turned towards the street. And in any case my decision was no more than a thought: At the end of this paragraph I'll get up and go out. As the thought crossed my mind Bobo would rise, stretch, and walk to the steps where it was his custom to sit beside me while I was resting.

When I was going to be away in the evening and could not take him, Bobo would be depressed all day, and when I would start preparations to go—the same preparations which at other times meant he could come—he turned his face towards the wall. If, however, I was going to be with a family that liked dogs and expected me to bring Bobo, his spirits rose steadily as the evening approached.

In some ways it was very convenient to have our communication so sensitive. But I never could fake an emotion with him (nor can I with Tunerak). Sometimes when the writing was not going well and I wanted to stay with my thoughts about it, temporarily I had no warmth of feeling to give anybody, including Bobo. I could talk brightly enough to fool people, apparently, but however great the attempt I could not convince Bobo. I could chatter and smile at him but the shadow of loneliness plainly lay on his spirit.

There is nothing in all one's association with a Husky dog that is more impressive, and more an influence, than his quick detection of insincerity. Politeness is not enough if it is only constructed politeness. Kindness won't do if it is no more than courteous manners. With Bobo I was reminded often of something that Eskimo mothers say to their children: "You must always smile at an enemy, and try to feel the smile in your hearts." If the smile that you give to a Husky does not come from the heart, he will know, and he would prefer that you not falsify the friendliness.

There were no tragedies in my life during those years, no distress more serious than minor disagreements with publishers or with the amateurs who were remodeling the house. In cases like those Bobo always sensed my concern and let me know he was sorry; I'd open a letter which stated that a manuscript had to be cut, certainly shedding no tears over such a small disappointment, but Bobo would cross the room, put a quick, delicate touch on my hand, and go back to his rug.

This kind of communication went on for years—seven years, even after Bobo and I had left Nome. I don't think of it as peculiarly a Husky talent. It's a familiar habit of dogs to post themselves in a window shortly before a master comes home —at a time that is not customary. Many dogs realize in advance whether they may accompany someone who will be leaving the house. The intuition of all animals seems to me to be marvelous, and equally astonishing is the fact that we take it for granted. We don't follow through on the implications.

Animals can receive, and give, impressions in ways that we don't understand. If the ability was sharper in Bobo, that acuteness may have been due to the fact that his mind was more wild. It is a wild trait: of that I'm convinced, having seen many signs of it in the wilderness where I have lived from time to time. Bobo's wild sensitivity was applied in human, civilized situations, and therefore it seemed spectacular. But most people who have congenial pets can communicate with them on a level of consciousness that does not require verbalizing. That experience may be one reason why the animals' company is so satisfying: they put us in touch with our human instincts, now nearly lost to most of us, and we feel we are in better balance, functioning more as whole people, when our own intuition is not so atrophied.

Any wild voice can stir something mysterious and exciting in us, and silent messages from a wild mind are even more moving. The human mind that receives them knows directly then what wildness is. The human being knows it because he himself is partaking a little of wildness.

I realize that ideas like these, as well as examples of Bobo's insight, will seem unconvincing to many. To them, their doubts; to me, who had the experience, my knowledge of what can happen.

13

It could almost be said that Bobo was starting to round up another pack, now of people. For a time it had only one member, myself. But Bobo was making a circle of human friends so devoted that he soon may have felt some sense of authority with them.

He still shunned other Huskies—even Polar had drifted away, and Bobo avoided all dogs except puppies, but most people liked him, and he was certainly not a one-man or one-woman dog. (That devotion to an owner exclusively may be a trait bred into dogs, since their wolf ancestors normally are more sociable.) I was glad that he did have an impulse to promote human acquaintances, because it was going to be necessary for me to leave Nome and Bobo soon. The separation was going to be temporary, but would the dog understand that? If he felt he was being deserted still another time, the confidence he was getting back slowly, after the fight, might be badly damaged.

He had a different kind of relationship with each of my friends, and it seemed often that Bobo took the initiative in forming it. He was always the one who approached them, whether in their house or mine, and he sensed whether a formal greeting was called for or whether he could be more spontaneous. The home where he was most like himself was that of Mrs. Omie McCarthy, a retired teacher who, at sixty, still responded to life with a joyous *Yes*. Bobo knew he was free there to satisfy his enormous curiosity; he looked into all the closets, under the beds, in the storeroom. I was embarrassed for him, but Mrs. McCarthy was only amused.

I don't know who gave him the name Bobo, but as applied to him it had style, for the dog had style, and it never showed better than when I was giving a party. He greeted each guest as if that were his responsibility, standing in front of the man or woman until he compelled a response. Typical was a gathering where the district attorney was telling a story when Bobo entered. Bobo walked over in front of him, listened until he was through, and then, with a slight lift of his head and a slight acceleration of his waving tail, showed that the time had come for their mutual greeting. Bobo went all around the circle and when each guest had been received, he attempted to entertain us by singing one of his more elaborate wolf songs. Sometimes on those occasions he would start a conversation with me, the human and Husky questions and answers that never failed to attract attention. Much of his act had that purpose of course, to be noticed, but some of Bobo's new friendships began at those times. He knew where my guests lived and would visit them by himself later.

He had other friends, some that I didn't know. One night at the camera club I met a stranger who said, "Your dog certainly likes pancakes."

"Pancakes! At home he won't eat anything but lean meat."

"I cook a stack of cakes for him every morning. Maybe I should give you my recipe."

One woman told me in a glow of generosity that she had

fed Bobo a whole turkey carcass. Since even one chicken or turkey bone can be lethal by splintering and piercing a dog's stomach wall, I sometimes wondered whether Bobo might literally be killed by kindness.

There were other dangers. A comparative newcomer called one day and began in a rather distraught way, "I've come to tell you that you just have to let me have your dog, Bobo. I'll buy him from you, but I just have to have him. There is a kind of bond between us."

I told her I knew what she meant because there was a kind of bond between Bobo and me, too, and I couldn't give up my Husky. But she wasn't dissuaded easily. With a husband who was a hunter, she had a cache full of wild game, and she used to entice Bobo indoors with it and keep him there. When my dog stopped eating at home, ever, I had to keep him chained up for a while.

One of the airmen based at Nome also decided that he "had to have" Bobo. "I just have to take him back to Caifornia," he said, "and you can name your price." The boy so earnestly felt that he had to have Bobo that I rather worried about what would happened when the boy rotated. Some of the town's finer Huskies had disappeared with the departure of troops. And just about the time that I knew that particular boy was due to leave, Bobo disappeared. I inquired around town, of course, and three tiny Eskimos, two and three years old, said that Bobo "got in car." That was all anyone could get out of them. The town police and the military police went to work; the airman had, in fact, left on the day Bobo vanished, and very co-operatively, the Base commander sent tracers after him.

On the third day of the dog's absence the trio of infants

came to my door and said, with their radiant Eskimo smiles, "We show you Bobo?"

Eagerly, in the spring sunshine, I followed the children to the waterfront and on up the beach to where, they admitted, they had shut Bobo up in an abandoned sedan. Ravenous and frantic with thirst, he bounded out of the car and home.

How wide was his group of friends I knew by the number of people who spoke to him on the street or if he was not with me, would ask, "How is that Bobo?" And their eyes as well as their lips would smile.

Bobo also was making enemies; were they the "outside dogs," outside of his pack of people? One was an Eskimo, the best carpenter I'd had work on the house even though he was seldom entirely sober. Bobo, however, disliked the man. When he was there Bobo stayed indoors and lay on the floor, never taking his eyes off the Eskimo. He didn't growl, snap, or show his fangs, but no one could doubt his feeling. Finally the carpenter said, "I am not going to work for you any more. I don't like the way your dog look at me."

Ann had told me that Bobo was antagonistic to any man who was drunk, and so I said to the carpenter, whom I wanted to keep on the job, "It might be the beer. If you would wait for your drinks until after work——"

"I don't want any dog telling me I can't have beers with my lunch."

I offered to chain Bobo outside during the day, but the man was not pacified. "He see me when I come and he see me when I go and he look at me in a mean way." The man quit.

Later I told that incident to an Eskimo woman I knew. I described it as something amusing, but the woman said,

"Bobo was right. That man steals. He boasts that he steals. He is not a good man." And then, after a thoughtful pause, "Dogs know more than people do. Dogs can see ghosts, too, and they can make them go away. When we are camping, if we think there are ghosts in that place, we bring one or two of the dogs into the tent, and then we feel safe."

There were two other men in town that Bobo disliked, triggering such reciprocal animosity that the feuds became rather alarming. I wouldn't suspect either man of stealing, and I have no idea what was behind Bobo's feeling. One was a taxi driver, an amiable fellow, an Italian whom everyone liked. I had been using his cab, and, since Bobo so loved to ride in cars I had been taking him to my destination, from which he would walk home. But this particular driver surprised me one day by saying, "This is the last time I'll come for you, because I don't like your dog." What had Bobo done? "Nothing, but he hates me and I hate him." It wasn't enough that I said I'd leave Bobo at home. The man said he didn't even want to stop in front of the house.

The other instance seemed just as irrational. One of Nome's better-known residents, a mine owner, kept taking Bobo to the police station, saying vaguely that the dog had caused trouble. Normally I would have had to pay a three-dollar fine to redeem him, but the police, all of whom liked Bobo, would bring him home on a leash and apologetically suggest that I keep him chained for a day or two. Once, more soberly, they reported that Bobo's enemy had said in anger, "The next time I catch that dog, I am going to take him out beyond the town limits and shoot him and nobody will ever know what became of him."

I shut Bobo up inside and went to the office of the Nome

lawyer to ask what I should do. A sharp little man, with a rough and ready approach to frontier justice, he swung his chair around so he could watch the Bering Sea waves break on the beach for a minute. When he turned back he said, "The fellow's got two or three trucks. If you were a man I would advise you to put sand in the gas tanks some night, but I guess you can hardly do that." I assured him I couldn't. Then he began scribbling a letter to the mayor. It stated that one of the councilmen (Bobo's foe) had threatened to kill my dog. Since Bobo was not in the habit of running away, if he disappeared we would assume that the councilman had in fact killed him, and we would sue the city of Nome for ten thousand dollars. The councilman was not named, but when the letter was read at the next council meeting, the members got a confession out of the one who had made the threat, and he gave them his promise to let Bobo alone. I knew the man slightly; he seemed stable enough, and I never attempted to speculate on the reason why he and Bobo disliked each other so much. I suspected that the unfriendliness had begun with that curious accusation which could come into Bobo's eyes.

Altogether happy, and rewarding on both sides, was Bobo's relationship with the children. Formerly, when he could spare time from his leadership of his pack of dogs, Bobo had played with them and they had sought him out almost as regularly as the Huskies did. In the usual way of little boys, those in our neighborhood went around in a crowd, and later Bobo was one of them—the only dog they took everywhere, although some of the boys had pets of their own. If they sat on somebody's steps, conferring, Bobo sat on the steps with them; if they got into a huddle over important plans, Bobo was in the center of it. They took him along on their exploring trips and down to the beach where they played ball at low tide. The schoolyard was only a block away from our house. By an animal's unexplained time-sense Bobo knew five minutes before the children came out for recess or were dismissed to go home, and he would trot over and be in the schoolyard a minute or two before the bell rang. Always and everywhere that one saw him with children, they were showing their fondness for him. A boy's arm would drop over his shoulders, a child's hand would curl one of his ears, they were smoothing his fur. On stormy days the doorbell frequently rang after school and one to three or four children would ask if they could "come in and play with Bobo." The play was not boisterous; the children, many of them the well-mannered little Eskimos, would stretch out on the floor looking at pictures in magazines with Bobo stretched out among them, and inevitably small brown fingers would be in his ruff.

Tunerak has the same affinity for children. When I drive along with him in the car, cries come from the youngsters we pass: "There's Tuno!" Tuno has a tremendous friendship with a two-year-old boy who is contented indefinitely if Tuno is near to lean against, to hug, to hang onto. With both dogs I have thought there was some correlation between their fondness for children and the fondness of all adult wolves for any puppies that belong in their packs. Did the dogs think of the children as puppies?

Ann said that Bobo had always enjoyed playing with puppies, a kind of recreation I would not have expected in an unmated male dog. In the spring after he came to live with me, as soon as the Husky litters were born and weaned, Bobo would get one of the tiny dogs somewhere and bring it home and play with it for the entire day, after which he would take it home again. No doubt the puppy satisfied one of his latent wolf instincts, and perhaps was the beginning of his return to Husky company. For, being Bobo, eventually he would have to try to win back his old place as the leader in Nome's dog community.

The book about arctic wildlife was finished, although some details had to be checked in a good biological library; and I had developed an intermittent fever that could not be diagnosed with the facilities at Nome. For those reasons it was going to be necessary to leave Alaska for several months. It didn't seem possible to take Bobo, since the Nome doctor predicted a stay in a hospital. I did plan to send for him if I should be away long, doing research, after I was well. In the near future, however, Bobo faced still another desertion.

The date when I'd leave would not be set till I found a tenant to live in the house and take care of Bobo. I hoped it would be someone who understood Huskies; if not, someone who would be interested in learning about this different and complex breed. In the meantime the lemming project was being brought to an end and summarized.

Over the many months of continuous watching and keeping of records, several facts had developed that could have a bearing on a few of the unanswered questions concerning lemmings.

The metered wheel had proved that there was great variation in their activity, or, as it seemed, their nervous tension, their restlessness. There was some indication that the weather might be an influence, but more definitely so was the phase of the moon. I had long known that I was apt to have migraine headaches near the time of the full moon, and here were my little lemmings, nearly going mad for exactly the same two or three days. They fought so frequently then that I kept a tub partly filled with water, in which I could put them to calm them (physical therapy); but it was the number of miles run in the wheel that furnished conclusive proof. They would run about nine miles per day per lemming under ordinary conditions, but half again as far just before the earth came into line between the sun and the moon. At that time, of course, the earth is subject to gravitational pulls in opposing directions, towards the moon on one side and on the other side towards the sun. Since those conflicting pulls are strong enough to cause maximum tides in the seas, it would not be surprising if they could be felt by the earth's living creatures. While I was doing research on the book at Harvard, I found impressive records that many living things do appear to be so affected—not only mice and human beings, but even trees in the speed of their growth. The significance in the lemming study lay in the possibility that if the animals' periodic frenzy were intense enough, one of those times it might set off the start of a migration. To watch the lemmings, one would say that they were hysterical then, and if out of doors they no doubt would be inclined to start running.

But why would they not simply run around aimlessly near their nests—why leave their familiar environment? I had a clue to that answer, too, in the fact that my lemmings could not tolerate more than a certain degree of crowding.

Again and again I tried putting more and then fewer of them into the big glass cage. In that space, approximately six square feet of surface, four lemmings would live with little discord, except when the moon was full. If I would add one more lemming from upstairs—any one of them—all five became desperate. Three didn't seem to get along in the cage any better than four; four appeared to be an acceptable population density. But five invariably caused trouble, and six or seven so disturbed one another that I never dared leave that many together for long. I lost two of the lemmings because the excess were not taken out in time, and the two died in fights (they were not the newcomers—the regular cage mates fought just as violently with each other when there were more lemmings than four).

Since it is known that the lemming population increases phenomenally every three or four years, it may be that then the profusion of lemmings reaches a number unbearable to them. When that happens, I suspect that the lemmings, always high-strung, would try to escape from the crowding that so offends them. When lemmings do migrate, they have an impulse to run *down*, and if they were attempting to get away from one another but were all running down, they would run together. Down the folds in the hills, down the dry creekbeds in summer, down gulleys, down valleys: they would be taking their scourge with them and their direction would bring them at last to the sea. That they would cross rivers easily in their flight was evident from their skill as they swam in the tub; and the ocean would look to them like only another, very wide river. Perhaps no one ever will know positively the reason why lemmings do migrate to the coastline and drown, but I had found with my little colony what to me was a satisfactory explanation.

There had been a chance to watch briefly a lemming from the *Dicrostonyx* species, the one whose members turn white in winter. Someone had captured it on the tundra near Nome and, knowing my interest, had given it to me. It was a young one and, compared with the young of the brown lemmings, was rounder in contour, with larger eyes and a shorter tail. It was golden and white in color with markings different from those of the immature brown lemmings.

For two or three days I kept this one alone, but he sank into that lethargy which nearly always is fatal to captive animals, and therefore I removed one of the regular lemmings from the cage and gave him its place with companions. The others were fairly friendly; they showed a few signs of antagonism, but not enough to seem serious. The new lemming climbed extremely well, he was almost a little acrobat, as might be expected of an animal born to scramble around in bushes. He apparently had no fear, no wish to be hidden, sleeping anywhere, especially up on a piece of driftwood. His voice was different from the others', being high and birdlike instead of a resonant chirr.

He was especially drawn to a large, slow, rather heavy lemming that I had thought of as a grandmother nearing the end of her life. The small one kept nudging close to her, even though she ignored him. One evening when she was asleep on the top of some moss, he crept up and lay against her side, going to sleep himself with his little paw clutching the grass stem that had been one too many. As I was watching them, hoping she might adopt him and mother him, she woke and without warning stabbed the young one's throat with her teeth. He darted away, thrusting his head and neck into some nearby mud, which might have stopped the flow of blood if it had not been too serious—but within a few seconds more he was dead.

Had she only been startled to find him there, or was it a

mistake to expect two slightly different species to inhabit the same territory?

Three of the lemmings regularly housed in the cage had died during the study and had been replaced from the group of the mother and her eight offspring. I had found one of the upstairs lemmings dead, apparently of wounds inflicted when fighting, since its throat was torn. The other lemmings had left its body alone; there never was any evidence of cannibalism among the lemmings, unless the second litter of young, born during the first summer, had lost their lives in that way. No other litters besides the two early ones ever were born in the colony.

One of the upstairs group was found, incredibly, on the studio floor. I discovered it as it was trying to climb out of the oil in a cakepan set under the line to the heater to catch a drip. I gave the lemming a bath in soapy water, but a day or two later it died and left unanswered the question of how it had got downstairs. Over the metal plate barring the doorway into the lemmings' room, and where the door itself always was closed? And then down the stairway and through an additional door that in winter was never open? Or had it fallen through the register in the floor that carried the downstairs warmth up into the lemmings' room? And if so, could it have survived a drop of ten feet? I wouldn't have said any lemming could possibly escape from that tightly sealed upstairs room, but here it was in the pan of oil.

Bobo was out when I found it. Later, when it was quite accessible in a box on my desk, he ignored it.

The departure of this one should have left four upstairs: of the original nine, three brought down to the cage, one killed, and one dead of its oil bath. What became of the final four never was known. I had heard them regularly, running about, spinning their wheel, chirring—and then from a certain day on there was silence. With the help of one of the Eskimo boys I cleaned out the room. We sifted the earth in which they had burrowed, almost stalk by stalk we removed what grass they had not eaten, we took out the pieces of driftwood one at a time. No lemmings were there. They were just gone—a fact to be added to the rest of the lemming mysteries.

The family that rented the house seemed quite satisfactory —a civilian engineer with the Army, and his wife, and two pleasant children, eight and ten years old. They were intelligent people who said that they would be glad to take care of Bobo. They never had had a dog and their children had wanted one. They would move into the house in about ten days. In the meantime I urged the boy and girl to play with Bobo. They did, and their mother told me they found him a little disappointing. They had expected that Bobo would romp with them, frolic as puppies do. I explained that the Husky temperament is more grave, that they are dogs bred to take responsibility. Bobo would want to be with the children and would love them but probably never would bound around, panting for their attention. Watching the little Eskimos would give hints as to how Huskies like to be treated. In my own mind I trusted Bobo to work out the relationships.

From the day the agreement was made with the tenants, Bobo showed that he felt himself an abandoned dog. Now the old loneliness never left his eyes. He made no more little affectionate overtures, never started one of our conversations. He never walked to the store with me; in fact he stayed away from the house much of the time. When he did come home, and lay down indoors, he turned away from me. His fur was becoming dull. And he ate less and less—sometimes nothing at all.

It was a difficult time for me, too, not being well and trying to arrange everything for an indefinite absence. And here was Bobo going into a fast decline before my eyes.

In associating with a very intuitive animal there is a special frustration when one reaches the boundary of his understanding. He can comprehend so much that it seems he knows everything; then one comes to the limit. Words could have bridged the gap, but our kind of communication is not carried on with words. Bobo knew I was leaving him, but in spite of all the times that I told him, and all the times I consciously tried to put the thought into his mind, he could not grasp the fact that I would come back or, if not, I would send for him. "I am not deserting you, Bobo. Some day we will be together again"—over and over I said it, but that projection of vague promises was beyond his grasp. He did know that I was going away and he would be left behind. Into a further future he could not see.

I was wrong, however, in fearing that Bobo would allow himself ever to pine away. He was acting already as if he no longer considered that he was my dog. He did come home every night, but not until bedtime, and he was gone in the morning as soon as I let him out.

I was to leave on the noon plane on Friday. On that day too Bobo had disappeared early, and I hoped that he might not come back while I was there. With the dog so misunderstanding the situation, the thought of the parting was almost unbearable.

It was a warm August day, and the front door was open as I completed the packing. At half past eleven then, as I stood in the living room waiting for a taxicab, Bobo appeared in the door. "Bobo——" I said, and took a step towards him. Bobo's eyes held on mine for a moment, so compellingly that I was reminded of the day when I told Ann I could not take him because of the lemmings, and Bobo begged that I let him live. What would I do now, if again he flung himself on my protection? Would he make one last plea that this parting should not take place?

No, for he has turned away, down the steps and the walk, and although, weeping, I called good-by to him from the doorway, he continued on up the street, not once turning his head to look back.

14

I was gone from Alaska for more than a year. The tenants were good about sending down news of Bobo: how he had adopted the engineer as his special companion and spent most of his days in the engineers' office. He loved to ride in their jeep. (Did he ever pass Spider and would Spider bark at *him?*) I sent Bobo some dog food for Christmas and enclosed a worn glove, hoping its scent would tell him I still was alive. His intuition at times had spanned several blocks at Nome. I doubted that it would reach to New York and Boston.

In those brisk and determined cities I often longed for the North, and I thought of Nome and how well it accommodates both a Husky dog and anyone who is engaged in such work as writing. Nome has a core of seriousness—without it nobody would survive long in that climate—but on the surface it has the spontaneity of the wilderness and of artists' Bohemias.

In all those environments, Nome, a wilderness, and Bohemia, the way to support oneself is by searching; and the difference between searching and, say, manufacturing is more pervasive than one might expect. The white residents of Nome search for gold and now other minerals; the other half of the population, the Eskimos, search for seals, crabs, fish, whales, and walrus. If you are going to build factories, buy raw materials and sell finished products competitively, you have to be able to drive yourself and your workers or probably you won't make a profit. But if you just hope to *find* something, and it might be almost anywhere on the ocean or tundra, or in the mind, you inhibit the forcing, the pressuring. You try to become patient, sensitive, and to blur, slightly, everything but this place and this moment. Those are some of the rules for success in following the nose.

Most of the little incidents in a scene like that of Nome will have bounce . . . because it's a curious thing about the searching temperaments that a kind of gaiety, joy, springs up without really adequate reasons. Such people, focusing on the immediate present with great awareness, notice the shimmering light on the Bering Sea, they feel the touch of the breeze on their skins, they see the patterns in blowing snow. They smell the bacon frying in some sourdough's cabin, they taste the salt from the sea on their lips, they hear the lilt in the children's voices, and in these quite simple things they are able to feel delight. The delight is apt to express itself by running a few steps in a mock chase of a child, or in stopping to scratch the ear of a friendly dog. And of course an animal like a Husky, whose inborn means of supporting himself is by searching, is wonderfully at home where the people too have an inner aliveness that is making their senses acute.

So it was that the urgency of the two very civilized cities made me homesick for Nome and for Bobo. I did go into a hospital, the convalescence was slow, and the final research on the book took more time than I had expected. When I saw that it would, I intended to send for my dog, and asked a veterinary what injections the Commonwealth of Massachusetts requires of an incoming animal. He strongly advised me not to bring Bobo down. The local dogs, he said, have diseases to which the Alaska Huskies are not immune. I would be very likely to lose him. I resigned myself to the further wait and sent Bobo my glove.

While I stayed in Cambridge to be on hand to correct the proofs of the wildlife book, I wrote an article about Bobo—not fiction, just a piece telling about his life and describing the kind of dog he was. I called it, "My Husky Trained Me." In Fairbanks, on the way back to Nome, a letter caught up with me from the editor of *The Saturday Evening Post*, saying he liked the article and in a few months would publish it.

Would Bobo remember me? I thought that he would. And also forgive me for leaving him? Of that I was not so sure. I would have to stay in one of the Nome hotels for two weeks till the tenants moved out of the house. Soon after the taxi left me there I walked over to Second Avenue.

Bobo was not in sight, but just as I reached my house he came from around the corner. I sat on my heels where I was and spoke his name. He stopped with his eyes on my face but seeming so dazed that I thought, He has forgotten. Then he rushed forward, bounding softly as in a dream, till his chest touched my throat, which was real—and his head, over my shoulder, pressed hard on the side of my head for two or three minutes. It was long enough for the human being and non-human being to measure their recent loneliness.

The hotel manager let me keep Bobo there—fortunately, because he came down at once with a serious illness. Dr. Kennedy thought that it was pneumonia. In any case it appeared to be complicated by Bobo's new, overwhelming sense of insecurity. I could not make him feel that I had come back to stay, and his great anxiety was an actual threat to his life.

In the hotel room he kept close to me; if I moved away from the spot where he lay, he hurried over to give himself reassurance by touching my hand. I sat on the floor through several nights, holding his head in my lap and at intervals pouring medicine or warm milk down his throat. Finally his fever broke and "You can begin to hope that he'll live now," Dr. Kennedy said. By the time we moved back to the house he was almost well.

I was eager to see what Bobo's relationship with the other Nome dogs had become. I had learned that Polar had died while I was away, and Tulle's master had moved out of town. But the other dogs? They seemed to be in our neighborhood fairly often. Bobo however preferred to stay indoors, even after my bags were unpacked at home and we were getting into our old, comfortable routine. But after a few more days he was willing to lie on the little porch at the top of the steps; and finally he felt that his happiness might be safe if he guarded it from the yard. But I still didn't know whether Bobo had won back his Husky companions, or was going to be permanently isolated from the dog community by the collapse of his leader-prestige.

One morning then, as I was typing, my eyes were drawn to the ceiling by a reflection, a waving pattern of light and shade. Was it—yes! Out in the yard a congregation of five or six Huskies were wrestling, tumbling, their tails whirling and swinging, slowly and gracefully drooping, to be flung up again, whipping from side to side. And Bobo lay on the boardwalk, rather remote, dignified, with the inevitable aloofness of leaders. . . .

During the next week I saw him fight other dogs twice. Both times he won, and perhaps the vanquished dogs would be added to his new pack. For he did have a pack again, not as large as it was before nor, it seemed, quite as faithful; and I was not sure how long Bobo could hold his authority over the other dogs. He was growing older, and with every year additional strong young Huskies would be a challenge. If they didn't have Bobo's instinct for leadership they would not supplant him, but if he fought them and lost, Bobo's other followers probably would desert.

There was a different element in his fighting now: his constant attempts to shield his once-injured eye. He tried to manoeuver so that he stayed on the right side of the other dog; in that way his right eye was not exposed to the other's teeth. He had had to abandon his fast, free way of changing strategy to outwit his adversary. Moreover, both the dogs that I saw him fight plainly sensed that his eye was vulnerable and consistently tried to reach it. Bobo still could win against any dog that was not as swift or as clever as he—but the time surely was coming when he would lose his status. I had hoped he could know again, even if only briefly, that he had supreme authority over the dogs in the town. Perhaps he could give up then and still feel that his life was worth living. But now it seemed possible that he never might have that triumph.

Spider was not yet accounted for. And I hadn't been able to bring myself to inquire whether he still was alive and at Nome. But the question was soon to be answered. On one day the Kassons, our neighbors across the street, moved out of their house to go down and live in Seattle; the following day brought the worst luck that could befall Bobo: the new people moved in, and they were the owners of Spider.

Spider himself arrived on one of the truckloads of furniture. I happened to be outside, relaxing on the steps briefly with

Bobo. Did Bobo at once understand the entire and disastrous circumstances? Perhaps not, but he quivered with nervousness and his sickening hatred of Spider, and he cried, the old anguished whimper, too faint for Spider to hear, but I heard it, so deep within him it seemed that his very heart wept. "Let's go inside," I said, and took Bobo into the house.

When I looked out the window, Spider was pacing the boardwalk across the street, fastidiously and possessively and with as much assurance as if he knew he was the one that now would be dominating this block.

I could sell my house; we could move to Fairbanks where I could write about Eskimos quite as well as at Nome. I could not bear to see Bobo watch his enemy taking over his neighborhood, making every hour a torment—or would leaving, in fact, be a suitable thing to do? Was Bobo the kind of dog whose pride should be saved artificially? The pride of a house pet perhaps, but the pride of a wolf? Nature herself does not often solve anything in so easy a way.

The next weeks were perhaps the unhappiest Bobo had ever known. There was no doubt of the fact that he was afraid of Spider, and both of the dogs certainly were aware that he was. Bobo abandoned the block to Spider and spent all of his days in a different neighborhood. Some of his new group of followers lived on that street. One could say that his small, loose pack simply had a new meeting place, but Bobo's leaving his own yard was of course a defeat.

Spider drained as much satisfaction as possible from the situation. Most of the time when Bobo was not at home he stayed on his side of the street, but not always. When Bobo returned he could never be sure that Spider would not be patrolling the walk in front of our house. I tried to make certain that Spider was not outside when I let Bobo go in the morning, but the two dogs did meet occasionally and then Bobo always retreated. Once Spider followed him into our house, all the way into the living room, snarling and showing his fangs. I drove him out with a broom.

I still hadn't decided whether moving away was the thing to do. What was involved was a Husky's honor, and when the Husky was Bobo that didn't seem a fantastic thought.

One day in midsummer Bobo and I went for a walk on the tundra. We followed a dirt road beside the dry bed of an ancient creek. It wound through low hills and marshy ravines where even the willow brush edging the creek didn't obstruct the view. The way that one's eyes could range over the wide, spacious land, over its rolling and treeless surfaces, seemed in itself like a kind of racing, free movement. This was a wolf's country.

Where the plants were the marsh type, they clustered up into hummocks. In them the birds were then nesting, and the permanent populations of tundra voles and perhaps lemmings had their homes. Bobo bounded away from the road, through the marsh grass to hunt for the mice. He was gone a long time. Occasionally I would see the white flash of his ruff, rising out of the sea of green sedges as he leaped on his prey; or the sedges would show a long ripple where Bobo was streaming through.

I sat down on one of the creekside boulders to wait, and when Bobo returned, by way of the creekbed, his nose was searching for other scents on the mud-caked pebbles—scents of ancient remains of fish? He stretched out on a nearby sandbar, not panting, not seeming tired, only enjoying himself, and his eyes, intensely blue and their pupils enlarged with emotion, did not even see me. Nature's excitements were in them, stirring him till he seemed as young and vigorous as he ever had been.

After a moment he climbed a knoll, and the instant he came to its top he froze, tall, still, and vibrant. "What is it, Bobo?" Leaving the knoll without even a glance for an answer, he galloped through an adjoining gully to a low cliff, an outcropping of rock. There, with the farther view, again he froze, ears, nostrils, even the tip of his tail pointing off toward a bench at the foot of the higher hills that surrounded the marsh.

He appeared all wolf, seeming coiled—nature's spring—for a leap across several miles to the place that the wind had shown him. What did he scent and now see? I went up to his lookout.

Against the green hillside there was a movement, a brown mass, thorny-branched on top, slowly shifting about. Binoculars gave what may have been almost as close a view as Bobo had: reindeer, several hundred that recently had been drifted down from the north by their Eskimo herder. I had known they were there but had not thought of the stimulation they might be to Bobo. Reindeer are beasts so closely akin to caribou that when caribou happen to pass, the herders all have a problem to keep the reindeer from running away and joining them. Caribou! Except during the lemming migrations, the prime prey of the Northern wolves. What old instincts were stirring in Bobo, what longings, what wildness? Wildness itself is a call, a yearning, a homesickness even in human beings at times. And surely to any Husky——

I spoke to Bobo, and he shifted, stirring impatiently at my intruding voice. A flock of young plovers rose out of the grass just below us. If Bobo saw them, he gave no sign. It would not be surprising if he left and took off to find and rout that reindeer band.

"Home now, Bobie? It is time for meat." *Meat* was a word he knew and if he was hungry at all, usually it would bring him indoors. Now it did bring out his tongue, to curl out over his lips in unconscious anticipation. I started back down the gully, still murmuring "meat," and was pleased that Bobo did follow. He walked on in the direction of home, a little ahead and not really with me. His eyes still could have been seeing the brown backs with the antlers above them.

Half a block from our house we would turn into another road. We came to the corner cottage and started around it, and only the width of the road away found—Spider!

He was standing, looking out over the schoolyard. Bobo froze, compressing into a second the slow approach that belligerent dogs usually make to each other. It was a second in which Bobo's blood-thirst for reindeer must have been transferred to Spider. And then Bobo sprang forward, so fast that his flying feet were not visible, he was only a streak of fur——

Spider turned just in time to receive the full impact of Bobo's weight. Both dogs went down, rolling along in the dust. In a whirl then they were up to start spinning about for the fatal advantage.

Every breath was a snarl, a snarl coming up to a screaming pitch, as the dogs fought all over the road, fur, gray and black, with the white feet of both dogs and Bobo's white ruff telling that one was down, now the other, but each up again instantly.

The action all seemed confused, grappling, biting, tearing,

without strategy or control, but gradually the manoeuvering became clear—Bobo's efforts to keep the scarred right side of his head in the clear, and Spider's attempts to reach it. Spider, again, was not trying to find Bobo's throat. Eyes were Spider's objective, with Bobo the injured eye, the side of his head whose blood Spider had tasted before. Spider was fighting low, twisting his head to try to come up under Bobo's chin, but Bobo's teeth closed on his ears and kept Spider from following through.

Suddenly then, with a brilliant right-about leap, Bobo gave up his protection of his right eye and spun around to face Spider. Spider had no defense ready at this surprising move. He straightened up, Bobo ducked and caught Spider's front leg in his jaws, flinging him onto his back. Bobo at once was on Spider's chest, then, and his teeth were in Spider's throat.

I had gripped the palings of a white picket fence as I stood watching in fascinated horror, though once, when Bobo was down, I had started forward to try to kick Spider off, to get between the dogs, anything to try to bring to an end the mutual murder. But then Bobo was up again, with his teeth in the fur of Spider's back and holding him immobile for an instant of respite. I returned to the fence and was there when the moment came that Spider was helpless.

With a human rather than canine instinctive urge, I thought Bobo would close his teeth on the throat of that long-hated foe, bringing a quick death to Spider. And Spider, all in an instant, did go limp, but not because he was killed—he was asking for quarter! In this wolf and dog code of decency, often the winner does, at the height of his frenzy, check the impulse to kill that has been driving him till that second. By giving up, by relaxing, in effect by saying to Bobo, I am your victim, Spider was begging for mercy. I saw it and understood it, incredulous. This enemy he had loathed so long was now helpless—and would Bobo give him his life? He would. Bobo backed away.

Spider turned himself over and loped down the road, and Bobo watched him go. Then he came to me; disheveled and covered with dust, and with blood oozing from a new, long tear across his scarred eye, he came, not weakly but willing to show how tired he was, and he buried his head in my skirt for comfort.

Spider's defeat did not at first make any spectacular difference in the adjustment between the two dogs. The difference was there; Bobo was no longer afraid of Spider, and Spider no longer tried to intimidate him. But Bobo and his pack still had their headquarters elsewhere, and Spider still seemed supercilious, though he didn't come onto our side of the street. If these results of the fight were not very tangible, there was another that I assumed, without being sure, was due to Spider's humiliation.

After several weeks the police shot him. He did not bite any child but he approached a group of several of them in what seemed a threatening way, and one of the mothers, alarmed, called for official help. Actually no dog that is even slightly irritable is tolerated at Nome. Northerners are so keenly aware of the danger of attacks by untamed dogs that even if one shows but a slight disposition to snap, and even if a child has provoked the dog's anger by teasing him, that dog must be put away. There are no exceptions and there is no leniency.

Fairly often it happens that an animal defeated recently

in a dog fight will seem to be in a surly mood. It might only be temporary, but the police do not wait to find out.

Almost all Spider's life at Nome had been a defeat, for, wanting to dominate, he had been able to gain no followers. He had had one great victory over Bobo, but when it looked as if he could humiliate Bobo indefinitely, his old rival subdued him and in the most definite way. One can only surmise what new stress there was, then, in Spider's temperament, but it is possible that Bobo had, all honorably, rid himself of his hated enemy.

15

One of the most endearing things about the brave little town of Nome is the way its residents try to forestall the winter loneliness they call cabin fever. Ever since gold-rush days they have held series of entertainments throughout the dark months: wonderful big community card parties, so planned that each player meets about fifty people during an evening; Christmas festivities that draw everyone into the sociability; and best, the Roof Garden Party, a carnival on which weeks of preparation are spent, so genuine in its warm gaiety that friendliness simply takes over the town. It is for everyone, whites and Eskimos and on at least one occasion a Husky dog.

The Garden Party began as a fantasy, a denial of winter. Always staged in December, when the sea would be covered with ice and the landscape with snow, and the thermometer would seem frozen itself, at perhaps minus forty, the women went to the Party in summer dresses, with lace hats and parasols; the men wore "ice-cream pants" and white shoes and straw hats; the decorations were flowers: everything possible was done to create the illusion that this arctic night was a southern July.

The whimsicality finally wore out, and the Garden Party now changes its theme every year. It is held in the school gymnasium and always starts with a show, written and acted by the Nome people, and ends with dancing and games, wheels of chance, raffles, refreshments, all as buoyant as a balloon. It's one of the pleasures to see the Eskimos enjoying themselves so deliciously in the white-man's kind of fun.

The year I came back from Boston the show that opened the evening was called a Studio Party. It was a gallimaufry of local talents, in which the various entertainers were supposed to be guests at an artist's studio and performing for one another. I was one of the guests, and, after a dance with the artist-host, I was drawn aside by him for a confidential (with microphone) conversation:

Fred Bochman, the host: I understand that next week *The Saturday Evening Post* will publish an article that you've written about life in Nome. What's the subject of it?

s.c.: A Nome personality—one you see every day.

f.b.: Let me try to guess who. Male or female?

s.c.: Male.

f.b.: Young or old?

s.c.: Well, he has some gray hair.

f.b.: How long has he lived in Nome?

s.c.: He was born here.

f.b.: A gray-haired resident who was born in Nome? There aren't many of those. I'll soon have his name.

s.c.: I'll give you another clue. His life had to be pretty dramatic to make a magazine article interesting.

f.b.: And next week he'll be our most famous citizen——

s.c.: Known to millions of people, from coast to coast.

f.b.: Lucky guy! I give up——

s.c.: Bobo!

Bobo was there. For this climax I'd brought him onto the stage. When Fred and I started to dance, unknown to me Bobo had trailed us, and when we stopped at the microphone he remained behind, out of sight at our heels. At his name the audience broke into applause, and Bobo, curious, pushed between Fred and me and walked out to the footlights. The electrician centered him in a spotlight, and the audience cheered and whistled and stomped. Bobo looked searchingly at the sweep of faces, perhaps trying to find those he knew. He walked a few steps to one side and the other, and as the clamor increased he put his head back and bayed a long response. And then there was truly a tumult, from an audience that no doubt believed Bobo had learned and rehearsed his performance. But it was all impromptu, and therefore a great lark for those of us on the stage.

Bobo's stunt was the evening's hit, and after the show, when the general entertainment began, he had a sample of the attention the future would bring him. As he moved through the crowded hall, everywhere people turned from their dancing and games and cake and turkey raffles to exclaim over "our most famous resident." They talked to him, petted him, gave him a taste of what it can mean to be a star.

Anybody who knew him well saw how immensely he was enjoying himself, and if some of us found him amusing, no one could laugh at him, for he never abandoned his dignity.

Periodicals don't reach Nome until several weeks after publication, but a few copies come in with the passengers on the planes. Those with the *Post* article about Bobo were passed from hand to hand, and his prestige among the human residents and the tourists took on what was to be its permanent shape.

It was not dogs, now, that joined us when Bobo and I walked on Front Street, it was the local and traveling public: "There's our Bobo!" "That's the famous dog we read about!" "Look at those stunning blue eyes!" "Hi, Bobo!" "Oh, is he handsome!" Bobo would stand receiving the tribute, his unwavering gaze on the human eyes, and then, always Bobo first, he would turn away to move off as though he had to be gone, now, on other business. He still was a leader in every detail of his manner, but dogs interested him less and less as among people he had a full triumph. Actually the experience of making numbers of human friends, during the time he had lost his pack, probably helped him to seem gracious and comprehending as he received the new admiration.

Needing to go to Anchorage for a week, I took Bobo, and there he appeared on television as well as having a write-up and picture on the front page of the Anchorage *Daily News*. After that further publicity we hardly could make our way along some of the Anchorage streets, so many people would stop us. I was amused at myself to find that I felt slightly jealous of Bobo, who was receiving all the attention. That I had written his story, as well as more than a dozen other *Post* articles on Alaska subjects, had no interest for anyone when I had that magnetic dog with me. I remembered how frustrated actors can be when they try to capture an audience while they are sharing the stage with a dog—some say that it can't be done. Yet the article had been true and unadorned, and to *be* something memorable is surely more important than to describe something memorable. My little jealousy therefore drained away, and I only was proud of my famous Husky.

Two years later Bobo and I moved to Fairbanks. On the day

that I sold the house Bobo sensed that a change was coming. Through the next weeks he seldom would leave the house or yard, but he was not feeling abandoned this time; he acted as if he just wished to be sure that he wouldn't be left by accident.

The time in Fairbanks rounded out his life with so many new things to see and do that, although he was growing old for a dog, Bobo seemed to be starting his life again. The things that have meaning only in dog terms are rather limited in their number, but there is no end to the things that a Husky finds stimulating—in Bobo's case, for example, a plywood Santa Claus and a mobile electric sign: he raised his voice to them, and I wished that I could interpret the comments. A Husky is like an intelligent small child first discovering what the world is like—one reason possibly why Huskies are apt to seem vigorous to the end of their lives.

Bobo never had seen trees before, and his tail flung around with excitement as he watched the birch and spruce boughs blowing, the birds flying in and out, and the squirrels running along the branches. He would bay at the squirrels, and they would come down the trunks and chatter, just out of reach. Then they would dash back up, jump to another tree and come down the trunk of that one, an experience that was completely new to Bobo and an almost intolerable challenge.

Fairbanks has planned ahead for the new residents who are augmenting its growth: its streets have been paved well beyond the distance at present built up, so that one can drive out a hundred roads and find at the end a wilderness so far untouched, a hilltop commanding a sweep of three hundred miles of snow-covered mountains, a riverbank mossy and green, a patch of wild berries, a woodland pond. In some of those woodsy havens the famous Alaska mosquitoes take possession, but for only about six weeks. During the spring, the latter part of the summer, the lovely fall, and about half the winter Bobo and I went out every afternoon, and while I sat in the parked car and rested, or worked on an improvised table, Bobo explored and found all the wild things he never had known existed. On the tundra surrounding Nome flowers grow in a few places but I don't believe Bobo had seen many of them. The woods around Fairbanks are virtually a garden, and Bobo proved to be like the bull, Ferdinand, very fond of the fragrance of flowers. He would wander about, sniffing each blossom before he began the more strenuous business of calling to squirrels or trying to dig out the burrowers.

In one place where we went Bobo had his first and, by choice, only encounter with cows. I let him out at the edge of a pasture, and, seeing cows grazing two hundred yards away, he streaked towards them so fast that I was afraid there would be a slaughter. Perhaps Bobo had had the same expectation, but the first cow he approached laid her forehead down on the ground and when he ran into it, lifted him with her horns and tossed him about ten feet away on the grass. Bobo came back to the car even faster than he had gone out and for the rest of the afternoon sat on the back seat, gazing out of the window at the parking lot of the Fair Grounds with apparently great absorption.

We lived on the ninth floor of a modern apartment building, and since the management allowed dogs, there were almost as many dogs as there were tenants. No others were Huskies, and Bobo could intimidate all of them with the exception of one handsome boxer. When they met in the lobby the two growled and threatened each other in the most vicious way, especially if human adults had their collars firmly in hand and the dogs had no real chance of reaching each other. But out of doors they once settled the question of which was boss. The boxer fled, and after that Bobo could bluff all the dogs he saw. Up to the very last days of his life, when he was so weak with illness that he could not have defeated a terrier, he had the satisfaction of feeling supreme in his world of dogs. He still had his commanding stance, with his chin over the other dog's neck, and his eye was the eye of a leader although his strength was not.

With me, too, he was still independent. In Fairbanks he did walk on a leash at first, so willingly that I am sure he felt safer if tied to someone. Brought up in Nome, where at some hours not a single vehicle moves, Bobo was finding the traffic in Fairbanks a little frightening. But soon he was used to it and then he enjoyed dashing in and out of the stream of cars. I never enjoyed watching him do it, but it gave him the feeling of freedom his nature seemed to require. In Nome there had been a few times, usually as we were entering the house, when Bobo suddenly gave me a look which plainly meant, "I've had enough of this placid, confining routine," and he had turned and trotted off and hadn't come back for several days. Once he did that in Fairbanks, too, and in a way I was glad. I didn't want Bobo to become, ever, an old man drowsy in spirit.

And he never did. I was writing under some pressure, trying to meet a deadline, and I therefore hoped to employ various youngsters who lived in the building to walk my dog. With only one, a sensitive, quiet lad, would Bobo accept the arrangement. He would go out once or twice with the other boys, but something they did or did not do was displeasing to Bobo, and after that he lay down on the floor when they came to the door to take him, and he paid no attention to my politely phrased urging that he should go.

Bobo too was polite. He would conform to my wishes almost always, but up to the end of his life there were other times when he still said *No*.

From the high windows of the apartment one could look down at night and see a straight strand of blue sodium-vapor lights stretching far out into the vast, dark wilderness lying between Fairbanks and other civilized cities. Sometimes I was homesick for those cities, just as, when I was there, I had been homesick for Nome, and I used to amuse myself by telling Bobo how we would start out on that long, long highway some day and drive for five thousand miles and then be in New York. People there would admire him, too, though best for him probably would be the many wilderness miles through the northern reaches of Canada. I would describe the baby bears that would cross the road, the swift rivers flecked with the gleam of fish, the white mountain peaks that would seem to tower right up to the center of the sky—and as I talked Bobo's plume would be swirling from side to side, seeming as eager as if he knew what all the words meant.

But we didn't start soon enough, and when the time came to go, Bobo was no longer there.

One evening, as I was reading, suddenly Bobo cried out in what seemed intense pain. He was glad, then, to have a comforting hand stroke his fur. After a few moments he could relax, and so the pain must have eased, but something was different after that night. Gradually he grew weaker, he ate less and finally nothing, and he preferred to lie by the hallway door, where there was a rather strong air-conditioned draft. Once in the elevator, the lobby, or out in the street, he seemed almost as alert as ever, though sometimes the walk from our door to the elevator was too long without a rest on the way. His eyes showed the greatest change. They were at once reaching out and withdrawing into an infinite loneliness, as if Bobo knew perfectly that our separation was coming, and meanwhile wished we might comfort each other for the inevitable sadness.

One Friday evening I took him for a last visit to Fairbanks' good and kindly veterinary, Dr. James Beckley. He examined Bobo and said, "I'm afraid that you have a very sick dog." I left Bobo with him and went back to the apartment, and the next day Dr. Beckley telephoned: "I have sad news for you this morning. Your friend——"

My friend: yes, Bobo was my friend, in a truer way than we sometimes mean when we call the dog species the friend of man. Many dogs besides Huskies, of course, have the integrity of their original wildness, but usually we mean by a friendly dog one that gives us absolute and uncritical loyalty. That quality, put into the dogs by ourselves through selective breeding, doesn't do credit to us, for it makes of dogs something like the all-giving mother image that requires nothing in return.

Bobo was generous, too—I never hurt him accidentally, as in stepping on his foot, that he did not turn to me instantly with forgiveness; but he was the more valuable friend because there was sometimes a reproach in the wild-wolf voice. The wild voice does not always say *Yes*, it says *Yes, if . . . : if* we are true, if we are sensitive, if we are patient, if we are just—if we fulfill these requirements of the instinctive morality, then the wild voice will finish, *I will be your friend.*

At the present time there is a tendency among philosophers and sociologists to belittle the abilities of animals, perhaps in order to reassure the often-insecure human ego. In many places we read of "the moral law that was born with man," "the conscience that sets us apart from the animals," "the great step that was taken when man emerged from the beasts." In the arguments that follow statements like these there always are errors of fact which prove that the authors simply do not know animals, nor in many cases even the results of experimentation and observation long accepted by the social biologists. In the words of Sir John Arthur Thomson, "Too often, in the things pertaining to man, the evolutionist relapses into creationism, trying to make faculties out of nothing." Of those who are scornful of primitive nature, he says, "There is no appreciation of the ubiquitous beauty and the almost universal healthfulness, no mention of the parental care, the mutual aid, the kin-sympathy that are so common, no discernment of the rewards of survival and success that have been given to the self-subordinating as generously as to the self-assertive." The animals do not need to think about such virtues in abstract terms in order to practice them, but we who do think in abstract terms can recognize the virtues as related to our own codes of morality: "The behavior of man differs in degree rather than in kind from that of the other animals," said W. C. Allee, perhaps the greatest of all animal sociologists.

"The animals have virtues: men have ethics," is another way the biologists sometimes say it. Both virtues and ethics rely on a combination of instinct and learning; in the ani-

mals' virtues, more of instinct; in men's ethics, more of learning, of ideas transmitted from other men. We are in danger
of scorning our own instincts, of trying to turn the moral process over entirely to the intellect. But thought is not always
dependable; by thinking we can argue ourselves away from
truth as well as towards it, whereas instincts in their pure state
represent the accumulated wisdom of the whole species—what
it found good, what enabled it to survive—and therefore instincts seem to be much more surely grounded than structures
built up out of words, which can change their meaning overnight and which may never, in all their use, mean exactly the
same thing to two different people.

The words we love at the present time are the words of
science, but they can be deadly words, for as Professor Leon-
ard T. Hobhouse has warned, "A scientific conception of the
universe may become, as in our own time, a basis of resist-
ance to the developed social conscience, and serve as a justifi-
cation for unrestricted selfishness."

To balance the scintillating theories that come from the
scientific laboratories, therefore, do we not need to have as
much personal experience with nature as possible? Not nature
in books alone, but the fur under the hand, the fallen leaves
under the foot, the wings guiding the eye? Nature alive and
functioning can provide a measuring stick against which to
test the compartmented theories of the scientific minds.

It would be a saner, more healthful world if everyone could
have in his life a part-wild, part-domesticated animal like
Bobo. The human being would change, unavoidably, in some
of the directions the animal led: towards greater sincerity in
relationships, greater sensitivity in communication, greater
tolerance, and the fine, wild justice that never allowed Bobo

to attack a smaller dog or to continue to fight one that had asked for mercy. These traits are the roots of our own morality, but the tree that has grown from those roots has developed some withered leaves and some dying branches.

With the help of two men who had been fond of Bobo, he was buried beside the winding, peacefully flowing Chena River, whose banks he had loved to explore.

There could be no more suitable epitaph for him than the words of Dr. Charles R. Stockard, the geneticist who knew dogs very well and who once said, "In the beginning it may have been dogs that domesticated men."